Thinking Th

General
Graham Slater

4. Why Evil and Suffering?

Thinking Things Through

Already Published

The Bible
C. S. Rodd

Worship
Michael J. Townsend

The Christian and People of Other Faiths
Peter D. Bishop

In Preparation

The Sacraments
Michael J. Townsend

Is There Life After Death?
C. S. Rodd

Thinking Things Through

4. Why Evil and Suffering?

C. S. Rodd

EPWORTH PRESS

All rights reserved. No part of this publication
may be reproduced, stored in a retrieval system,
or transmitted, in any form or by any means,
electronic, mechanical, photocopying, recording
or otherwise, without the prior permission of the
publisher, Epworth Press.

Copyright © C. S. Rodd 1998

ISBN 0-7162-0518-1

First published 1998
by Epworth Press
20 Ivatt Way,
Peterborough
PE3 7PG

Typeset by the author
Printed and bound by
Biddles Ltd
Guildford and King's Lynn

Contents

General Introduction   vii
Introduction   ix

Part 1. Tragedy Demands an Answer

1. A Sad Birthday   1
2. Why are there Disabled Babies?   5
3. Two Visitors   10
4. Stephen Calls   15
5. An Evening with Geoff   19
6. A Further Tragedy   23
7. A Long Talk with Liz and David   27
8. Dr Mac   30
9. Geoff has a Get-together with a Few Friends   34
10. Anne has More to Think About   38
11. Not in Our Little Town!   42
12. An Evening with Geoff, David, and Fred   46
13. Anne and David Turn to the Bible   49

Part 2. Thinking Through the Issues

14. Sorting out the Problem   55
15. Some Dead Ends   61
16. Two False Trails   67
17. The Freewill Defence   72

Contents

18.	Natural Evils	76
19.	A Vale of Soul-Making	82
20.	Does God Intervene?	86
21.	People Before Doctrine	90
22.	A Suffering God?	93
Further Reading		97

General Introduction

The great German theologian, Hans Küng, has said that his aim in all his writings is to enable his readers to hold their faith with confidence and not with a bad conscience. This new series, prompted by the conviction that Christians need to think through their faith but often lack appropriate help in so doing, has a similar aim. Moreover, the assistance that it seeks to offer is related to another conviction: that many church members need persuading that theologians are concerned in any way with their problems and that theology can be at all relevant to their lives.

In such a situation, it is essential, we are sure, to begin with life and with church life. Only in that way can we be confident that we are dealing with grassroots issues. Plainly, however, it is not enough to identify the questions where they arise; we must also indicate the sources of help – if not of all the answers – in as non-technical a way as possible.

In some volumes, these tasks will be tackled in sequence; in others, they will be interwoven. Whatever the precise format, however, our hope is that, through this interaction, difficulties will be faced, fears dispelled, open discussion promoted, and faith informed and strengthened.

The books can either be read by individuals on their own or used in groups. We hope the questions at the end of each chapter will be useful both as a check that the text has been understood and as a spur to reflection and discussion.

Later volumes will deal with such issues as the sacraments, life after death, Jesus, the Holy Spirit, creation, salvation and discipleship, prayer, making moral decisions, science and religion, and presenting the gospel.

GRAHAM SLATER AND C. S. RODD

Introduction

Those who have read the first book in this series (on the Bible) will already have met Anne and some of her friends. They are not members of discussion group or a house fellowship, but just five friends who belong to the same church. But this volume is free standing, and can be read without any reference to the previous book.

When Anne discovers that her friend Liz cannot cope with looking after her little son who has Down's syndrome, she is immediately faced with the question, 'Why does God allow children to be born with such disabilities?' Other tragedies hit the church and the little town where Anne lives. The doctor son of one of the church members is killed by an earthquake in India. A friend is told that she has cancer and has only two years to live. She believes that God is punishing her for a sin she committed as a young woman, and her husband loses his faith because he cannot bear the loss of his wife. And a kindly old man is beaten to death in his own home.

In the second part of the book there is a more systematic discussion of the problem of suffering, picking up the doubts and proposed answers that were thrown up in the first part.

I wish once more to express my deepest thanks to Graham Slater for suggesting this series and for his constant encouragement during the time of writing this book. He has been a most enthusiastic supporter and gentle but firm critic of my style. Without him it would not have been written. I must add that I alone am responsible for the ideas expressed in it.

C. S. RODD

Part 1

Tragedy Demands an Answer

1

A Sad Birthday

It was just two years since Anne's friend Liz had had her baby. Little Simon suffered from Down's Syndrome. While Liz was pregnant the specialist had warned that he would probably be a Down's baby, but he was more disabled than Liz had expected. Anne noticed that Liz came to church far less often since he had been born. Once she asked whether there was anything she could do to help – baby-sit, perhaps, so that Liz and her husband, David, could go out for an evening together – but she was told very firmly that they could cope, thank you very much. She hadn't dared to ask again. Now Liz didn't come to church at all.

Anne had sent a birthday card on Simon's first birthday, but received no reply. It seemed as though Liz wanted to cut herself off from all her friends.

Now it was Simon's second birthday, and Anne determined to go round to the house.

At first she didn't think Anne was going to open the door, although it was quite obvious that she was in. When she did at last come, it was no longer the happy and thoughtful friend she had known from their schooldays. 'Oh, it's you. I suppose you had better come in.' Anne realized that something was wrong as soon as she saw Liz. She hadn't bothered to make herself up – she had always been the smartest girl in the church. When she reached the sitting-room Anne saw at once that it was serious. Little pieces of torn-up birthday cards were scattered all over the floor. There was no sign of Simon. And when Anne asked how he was she was met with a brittle, 'Upstairs, asleep.'

They sat in silence for some minutes, and suddenly Liz burst into uncontrollable sobs. Anne let her cry until she had worn herself out, simply putting her arm round her shoulder. At last, with swollen eyes and hard nose-blowing, Liz told her story.

Why Evil and Suffering?

David had wanted her to have an abortion. 'What kind of a life will it have?', he had said. 'How will we cope?' 'Will it be fair on any other children we may have?' The doctors had all advised an abortion. But she had held out against it. She felt that she simply couldn't kill the baby inside her. The baby was a person, not an 'it' as David insisted on calling him or her. It wasn't that she could find any direct teaching in the Bible against it. She just knew that it would be wrong for her to do it. It would be murder.

But it had all gone horribly wrong. She thought that she could love the baby, however disabled or even deformed he was. But she couldn't. She had looked after him lovingly at first, but soon she was leaving all the caring to David. Curiously, he was quite different now that Simon was there. He had set out all the difficulties when he had tried to get her to have the abortion. Now he couldn't spend enough time with him. He was always ready to change his nappy, to wash him, to put him to bed, and he spent hours just cuddling him whenever he was at home.

The crunch came with Simon's first birthday. She had got to know three other young mothers in the maternity ward and they had kept in touch. One of them suggested that they should have a joint birthday party, even though their babies weren't all born on the same day. She made a cake. They all went round to her house that afternoon. And Liz realized that Simon wasn't like the other children. He never smiled. He couldn't say 'Dadda' and 'Mamma'. He didn't crawl about on the floor as they did. She went home after that birthday party and decided that she would shut him away. Never take him out. Do only the absolutely necessary things. David would have to look after him.

Then the cards had arrived for his second birthday. She had started to put them up, then suddenly she had snapped. She tore them into tiny pieces and hurled them on the floor.

It was the first time she had spoken to anyone like this. Now she had started she couldn't stop. Why had God allowed Simon

A Sad Birthday

to be born abnormal like this? What kind of a world was it that God had made? How could you call God a God of love? She hated him. She didn't believe that he existed, but she hated him. Everything that those people at the church said was nonsense – cruel nonsense. God was a demon. He must take a delight in torturing people.

Anne let her talk. Then she quietly said, 'What about David?'

Liz was silent. It was clear that their marriage was near to breaking. Once they had been so happy, so very happy. Now they were like strangers, just happening to live in the same house and hardly noticing each other.

Anne encouraged her to talk. It seemed that David had never really believed that there was a God. He came to church because Liz came and he wanted to please her. He didn't believe that there was any life after death. He had urged Liz to have the abortion, because he didn't believe that the baby in the womb was a real human being. It only became a person when it was born and had life of its own. And yet once Simon had been born he had looked after him with such complete devotion. 'All his love goes there,' Liz said bitterly. I don't count any more.

Just then they heard the front door open and David came in. He was surprised to see Anne, and she thought she had better leave, but David said she must stay and see Simon. He bounded up the stairs and came down with the little boy in his arms. After he had shown Simon to her, he got his food ready and started to feed him.

It was quiet and it gave Anne the chance to ask the question that she knew she must find the answer to. Very hesitantly, she looked at David and said, 'So you're glad that Liz didn't have the abortion, after all?' He blushed, and said, very softly, 'It isn't easy to answer that question.' They were silent for some time. Then he said, 'I suppose you want to know what has changed my opinion.' And he went on to explain.

He hadn't really changed his ideas at all. He still didn't believe that there was a God. 'This world is all there is, and we

Why Evil and Suffering?

have to make the best we can of it,' he said. Perhaps the best thing would have been for Liz to have had that abortion. But he wasn't sure now. Life would have been a lot easier. And they might have had another baby who was healthy. But now Simon was here, and he and Liz were his mother and father. Simon belonged to them. He loved Simon. There was no one to blame for his being a Down's syndrome baby. It was just part of life as it chanced to be. The only humane thing to do was to care for him just as you would care for any other child.

They were silent again, and after a bit Anne gave both Liz and David a hug, touched little Simon's cheek, and left.

She had much to think about.

Questions to ponder and discuss

1. Why do you think David was able to accept Simon when Liz couldn't?

2. What answers can you give to the questions which Liz asked on pp. 2–3?

3. Whose 'fault' was it that things went so horribly wrong with Liz and David?

2

Why are there Disabled Babies?

Anne couldn't sleep that night. She kept on seeing Simon's impassive face, his father's eyes as he cuddled him, and Liz's tears – and the hard look that returned as soon as David came into the room. Worst of all, she remembered the floor covered with those torn up birthday cards. Again and again she was in that room, among all those little pieces of paper.

She still believed in God, but it seemed far harder now than before she had gone round to Liz's house. She would have to talk to Geoff.

She spent a miserable day, wondering how she could believe any more. Everything was so blank.

Fortunately Geoff was on his own the next evening and invited her round as soon as she phoned. She told him what she had found at Liz's, and all about Liz and David. 'Which of them is right?' she found herself asking. 'Is there a God? And if there is a God, why did he allow little Simon to be born as he is, and blight Liz and David's marriage?'

Geoff didn't give a direct answer. Instead, he asked, 'What would you have wanted God to do?'

Anne was quite sure that she could have made a better job of creating the world than God had done. 'There's no need for babies to be born deformed and with Down's syndrome,' she almost shouted. 'There's no need to have a world in which there is cancer, and pain. The world itself is completely deformed as well as the people in it.'

Geoff smiled that smile of his that could be so reassuring, but also so infuriating. It annoyed her now. 'You think I'm setting myself up as cleverer than God, don't you?' she burst out. 'Well, I'm sure I could have done better when it comes to all the evil in the world.'

Why Evil and Suffering?

'And isn't that the same as thinking that you are cleverer than God?' he replied quietly. 'Let's go over again what the three of you think.'

'Liz isn't sure whether there is a God or not, but if there is she pictures him as a divine torturer. David believes that there is nothing beyond this universe at all – you just have to make the best of it as it is.' He looked straight at Anne. 'And what's your position? It seems to be that God isn't exactly malignant but is certainly incompetent!' He paused. Then he went on: 'Well, at least all three of you have been honest. And you and Liz have been unwilling to let God off the hook. That's a promising start.' And he smiled again, and this time Anne found his smile soothing.

'But where do we go from here?' she said. 'We can't all be right. And none of the ideas that any of us has put forward so far seems particularly Christian.'

'Ah,' said Geoff, 'perhaps we should ask Stephen.' Anne was going to say, 'Not Stephen!' but before she could object, he picked up the telephone and was inviting Stephen round. 'Why not bring Frances as well?' he added. 'I can rustle up some supper and it will be nice to get together again. He turned to Anne. 'I know you think that Stephen is beyond the pale because he left us to join that fundamentalist sect, but we ought to listen to what he has to say. And we might as well see if Fred can come as well. I think it will be nice to get together again after all this time,' and he tapped out the numbers.

After the tremendous row they had had over whether the Bible was the word of God, Anne was a bit afraid of Stephen, but there was nothing she could do to get out of meeting him now. As it turned out, he and Frances seemed extremely pleased that Geoff had asked them round, and both of them shook Anne's hand very warmly. Fred arrived soon after. He was always glad to meet his friends and came in with his usual pleasant smile.

Why are there Disabled Babies?

They settled down to coffee and the wonderful cakes that Geoff baked, and then Geoff briefly set out the problem. He didn't give all the personal details that Anne had told him, but presented the bare fact that many deformed and disabled babies are born. How can we reconcile that with our belief in a God who loves all his children?

Stephen had a quick answer. 'It's because of sin,' he said.

Anne jumped in, more fiery than she had intended to be. 'Are you saying that the babies have sinned and that is why they are born like that?' Geoff gave her a look, and she went on rather more calmly, 'I mean, Liz's Simon was born with Down's syndrome. It wasn't his fault. He hadn't sinned. Or perhaps he sinned in a previous incarnation,' she added.

Stephen looked shocked. 'I don't believe in any of that eastern nonsense, as you very well know,' he said. 'No, I mean that we are all sinners because of original sin. Eve sinned, and led Adam into sin, and that sin has infected the whole human race.'

Geoff knew that Anne was about to deny that Adam and Eve ever existed and say that everyone with any sense knew that we had evolved over a long period of time, and he interrupted quickly to stop the conversation getting diverted into a different subject. 'But that still doesn't explain why Simon has Down's syndrome, while most babies who are born are perfectly normal, with healthy bodies and sound minds. The problem, surely, is why one is picked out rather than another.'

Stephen replied that this showed God's generosity. 'We all deserve punishment, but God is merciful and doesn't demand the full penalty from all of us during this life. But only those who believe in the blood of Jesus shed on the cross will be saved from the punishment of hell.' 'What a horrible idea!' said Anne.

Anne was even more troubled by Frances' response. She said that the Bible teaches us that God's ways are not our ways and that we cannot understand his purposes. If we are real

Why Evil and Suffering?

Christians we shall accept that what happens to us is for our best good. Anne burst out, 'But that means that what is evil to us may be good to God, and what we regard as good may in fact be contrary to his will!' She was going to add, 'What nonsense!' when she caught Geoff's eye and choked it back.

Geoff agreed that there is mystery in God and that we cannot know his complete will. There was a naughty twinkle in his eye as he said this, and Anne suspected that he was having a dig at those members of Stephen's church who seemed to know exactly what God's will was. Stephen hadn't noticed and went on with what to Anne was only rigid and cruel dogma. 'When Adam sinned, sin spread like a virus and infected the whole universe. The Bible says: "The whole creation groaneth and travaileth in pain together until now." We lost paradise and when God said to Eve that women would now suffer great pain in bearing children and told Adam that the ground would bring forth thorns and thistles, this shows us what a fallen world is like.'

Fred had been silent up till now. Anne was surprised, because she had expected that he would support Stephen and Frances, yet he was plainly getting more and more troubled by what they were saying. At last he spoke. 'I love the Bible,' he said, 'and I love Jesus. There are many things in the Bible that I don't understand, and I don't understand many things that happen to people in this life either. But I trust Jesus, and when I don't understand something I say to myself, "What would Jesus have said?"' He went on to explain that he didn't know why Simon had been born with Down's syndrome, and he was sure that Jesus wouldn't have said that it was because of the Fall. 'We live in a fallen world, but I don't believe that Jesus would have said some of the things that Stephen and Frances have just said. In the end I find I just have to trust Jesus and try to show the same kind of love to other people that he shows to me.'

After that there seemed to be little point in continuing the discussion. They had their own very firm ideas and the more

Why are there Disabled Babies?

they talked the more fixed those ideas became. Anne didn't believe that there ever was a historical Adam and Eve, and wasn't prepared to accept that Simon was simply part of a universe that had been corrupted by human sin. Stephen said that she wasn't a real Christian and they would pray for her, that she might find the Lord Jesus as her own personal saviour. But as he went out Fred squeezed Anne's hand. 'Don't stop trusting Jesus,' he said.

After the others had left Geoff gave Anne a grin. 'Well,' he said, 'we know where they stand.' Anne was completely exasperated, and in no mood for such casual mockery. 'I don't want to be prayed for, if it's going to make me like those two,' she said. 'I find their attitude to Liz's distress quite fiendish. They've got it all sewn up. They have an answer to everything, and don't see how cruel it all is.'

Why was it that discussions like this always seemed so unsatisfactory? No one was ever prepared to be convinced by other people's arguments. Some didn't even listen. And sometimes Geoff seemed just to stand aloof from it all. Was it just a game to him? She wasn't sure. She had come so eager to talk things over, but it had all gone wrong. As she went home she felt hollow, empty, and worn-out. It looked as if she would have another sleepless night.

Questions to ponder and discuss

Think about the positions adopted by Stephen, Liz, David, Fred, and Anne. Which of them is closest to your own beliefs? In what ways does your faith help you to understand Simon?

3

Two Visitors

The next day Anne was surprised by two visitors. First, Liz arrived in the morning. 'I hope you don't mind my coming,' she said, 'but I just had to thank you for all the help you gave me yesterday.' Anne wasn't aware that she had given any help at all, but Liz explained that it was the first time she had been able to tell anyone exactly how she felt. 'I haven't changed my mind about anything,' she said, defensively, 'but it was such a relief to be able to say what I did. You were so good.' They chatted together for a bit, and Anne promised to come round to see her again.

The other visitor was even more unexpected. That afternoon Frances presented herself on the doorstep. 'I must talk to you,' she said.

It was a long story, told with hesitation and embarrassment, and it took Frances a long time to get to the point. In the end Anne discovered that Frances had a lump in her breast. When she first discovered it she had prayed and expected it to go. She really had faith that God answered prayer. But it hadn't gone. It got bigger. 'It's God's punishment, that's what it is,' she said. And then she told her story. Before she had started to go out with Stephen she had had another boy friend. They had kissed and cuddled, and he had fondled her a bit. (It all took a long time in the telling, and there were many pauses.) One day they were alone in his house, and the kissing and cuddling had gone too far. 'You know how it is,' Frances said. 'Now God is punishing me. My sin has found me out at last. It's just like the Bible says.'

Suddenly she became frightened. 'You won't tell Stephen, will you? He'd be furious. I know he would. He's always been so jealous.' Anne assured her that it would never have crossed her mind to breathe a word to anyone. She certainly wouldn't break a confidence. 'But,' she told Frances,

Two Visitors

'you really must go to a doctor, and you must tell Stephen what the doctor says.' Frances was still worried about what Stephen would say. 'He'll question me. I know he will. He will try to worm out of me what sin I have committed to get this punishment.' Anne was horrified, but tried not to show it. 'I'm sure Stephen loves you,' she said, 'and he can't really think that the lump in your breast means that you have committed some great sin.' Frances didn't reply, and Anne realized that that was exactly what Stephen believed.

When she had gone Anne sat down to think it out. She was pleased that Liz had come and that she wanted them to meet again. She was also rather pleased that Frances had felt she could come to her with her troubles. But the two visitors had only made it all more confusing. She was coming to realize more and more that it wasn't just a matter of thinking out a problem. It wasn't just an intellectual puzzle. Liz and Frances were people with emotions as well as beliefs. It wouldn't be enough simply to discover the right 'answers', even if you ever could find them. For herself, she needed to think her way through rationally – she had to if Christianity was to make sense – but for those who were touched by the suffering it was quite different.

'People will say that they need counselling,' she thought to herself, and frowned. She didn't like the idea. It was as if they were a car engine that needed 'tuning'. In any case she felt it didn't fit. She wasn't a 'trained counsellor' and yet Liz had made the great effort of coming round to tell her how much help she had given her.

When she thought about David and Simon, however, it looked different again. It was almost as if David, the humanist, the one who didn't believe in God and who had only come to church to please Liz, had the best of the deal. Religion only seemed to make things worse for Liz and Frances, and as for Stephen – she gave a little shudder. His religion seemed so

Why Evil and Suffering?

twisted. How could anyone be so lacking in ordinary human kindness?

Fred was different again. He believed many of the things that Stephen and Frances did, but it didn't make him harsh and unfeeling. He was so kindly and considerate, and frankly, simply 'good'. Even though he believed that we were all infected by Adam's sin, Jesus meant much more to him. He trusted in a loving God who had sent Jesus into the world. Anne paused. No, that wasn't right either. Fred believed that Jesus was God, and the love that Jesus had was God's love. And on the cross it was God who was suffering for us. That made it so different.

But David. David just took the world as it was. Because he didn't believe there was God, he didn't waste time trying to explain why God should allow suffering. He just accepted things as they were and bent all his efforts on making it a little better. Life was pretty grim – 'It must be sheer hell for him sometimes,' Anne said to herself – but then she remembered how he had bounded up the stairs to fetch Simon and how he had looked at him when he brought him down to show her. 'He really is a good man,' she found herself saying.

Suddenly Anne remembered Monica. Monica had been a year ahead of her at school, but in the sixth form they had become great friends. Monica was the clever one. Ten 'A's at O level, four 'A's in A level, a place at Cambridge to study medicine, then on to one of the most famous teaching hospitals. All along the way she had carried off almost all the prizes there were. She became a consultant, and then headed a team of researchers who had made a major break-through in the treatment of cancer. And with it all she was still the same Monica, with great zest for life and always finding time for her friends. The only thing that separated her from Anne was their religion. Monica decided very early on in her school career that God didn't exist. It was partly the influence of one of her biology teachers. But she also said that she had never had any religious

Two Visitors

experience. 'If there really is a God, surely he would make contact with you.'

Then she herself had developed cancer. It was a particularly nasty kind, for which no operation was possible and which Monica knew would lead eventually to very great pain. Her attitude had astonished Anne. There was no bitterness. She never asked why it should have happened to her. Instead she began to look at herself as another medical case. She once said to Anne: 'It is so interesting to see how the cells work.' She persuaded her colleagues to try out a new treatment which was so novel that it would be years before they would have been in a position to test it on human beings. She kept full case notes – all the more valuable because she could monitor her body throughout the day – and often through sleepless nights – and could also write down exactly how she felt. Towards the end she had kept a careful record of the various ways they had tried to control her pain. When she died she left a body of evidence which one of the other consultants said provided them with a mass of data which could only have been built up by a vast amount of painstaking research.

Monica had no sense of God at all. The world of animals and human beings was simply as it had evolved. It was all chance, and the only worthwhile thing to do was to try to understand it better so that you could improve it a little before you died. And then you made way for other people to follow you. Death was entirely a natural and entirely necessary part of life. And she had died in complete peace.

Did religion only make things worse? The more Anne thought about Liz and David, Stephen and Frances, the less sure she was. Only Fred enabled her to keep her faith.

Why Evil and Suffering?

Questions to ponder and discuss

1. Why were the reactions of Stephen and Fred so different when they both believed the same things about sin and the cross of Christ?

2. What is your reaction to the view that suffering is God's punishment for sins we have committed?

3. Think about some of the people you have known who have been faced with suffering, either their own or someone else's. Did their religion make things better or worse?

4

Stephen Calls

It was nearly a month later. Anne was listening to her beloved Bach when the door-bell rang. It was Stephen. A very distraught Stephen. She had never seen him so wretched. Quickly she made two cups of coffee and sat quietly to listen to what he had to say.

He was almost incoherent at first. All he could manage was, 'Why didn't she tell me?' It took a long time before he said enough for Anne to piece together what had happened.

Apparently Frances had gone to the doctor as Anne had told her she must. He had sent her immediately to see a specialist, who had confirmed that it was cancer. But it was worse than she had imagined. The cancer cells had spread into the bones. The most they could do was to give chemotherapy. Frances had asked how long she had to live, and when the consultant was convinced that she really wanted to know, he had said that you could never tell, but he would say about two years. There was likely to be a remission for a time. They would do their best to keep it at bay by chemotherapy, and certainly would be able to control the pain. But the disease would win in the end.

Stephen kept on saying, 'Why didn't she go to the doctor before? Why did she hide it? She must have known something was wrong.' Anne tried to tell him that often there were no obvious symptoms, and she told him about one of her friends at work. This friend didn't know she had advanced cancer until she went to the hospital for something quite different and it was discovered almost by chance.

Stephen didn't seem to be listening. It was as if the bottom had dropped out of his world. This was no longer the man who had a ready-made answer to every problem and who knew exactly what God was saying and doing. 'She means everything to me,' he repeated again and again. Curiously he didn't say,

Why Evil and Suffering?

'Why does God allow it to happen to us?' It was as if his God had died with the cancer that had attacked his wife.

Because Anne didn't know what to say, she said nothing. At one point, when he was shaken by sobbing, she put her arm round his shoulders. After a bit he said, 'Thank you for listening. You're a good sort' – and left.

How strange people are, Anne thought. I would have expected Stephen to have got together all his friends in his church to hold prayer vigils. He seems just to have crumpled. I wonder what those friends are doing right now.

At her own church next Sunday Anne discovered that the news about Frances had got round. Some of the members were arranging a prayer group, and had set up a forty-eight hour prayer vigil. Everyone in the congregation was expected to join in. There was a list at the back of the church with half-hour slots in which to sign up. Anne wasn't at all sure about it but felt that for Stephen's sake she ought to add her name.

When she took her place in the upper room that they had set aside for the vigil, Anne wasn't at all surprised to find a set of Bible passages written out: the parable of the widow who pestered the judge until he heard her case, several of the stories of Jesus' healing miracles, Jesus' teaching about prayer and the way God gives good gifts to his children. She found it distracted her. Questions came into her mind. Did she really believe that Jesus had raised that widow's son from the dead? Did she really think that God would be persuaded to heal Frances just because of the forty-eight hours of prayer? She knew that deep down she didn't. This parade of prayer was futile if it was expected to change God's mind or make him do something which he hadn't thought of doing. What she had wanted to do was just to think about Frances and Stephen in their distress and quietly sit there with God.

Soon after she got back home there was a ring on the bell. It was Stephen again. He looked even worse than the last time she had seen him, and she quickly invited him in and made the cups

Stephen Calls

of coffee. She certainly needed the coffee herself – and it gave you something to do with your hands.

Again it took Stephen a very long time to explain why he had come and what the trouble was. When he had gone, after again thanking Anne for all the help she had given him, she sat in the growing darkness thinking and wondering.

She discovered that Frances had told Stephen about that boy she had known before they had got married. But, strangely, that wasn't what was bothering Stephen. He was too overcome with anxiety and grief. What troubled him was the attitude of some of his friends and the state Frances was in.

It seemed that one of the members of the church that he had joined when he left her church had come round one evening and told Stephen and Frances that they weren't real Christians. If they had been they would have cast it on the Lord in prayer and he would have healed Frances. They didn't have faith. That was the trouble. The church member brought a tract and solemnly read it out to them there and then. Then she had prayed with them and left, telling them that in spite of their lack of faith, she and her fellow believers were praying for them in the church and she hoped that they would soon return to Christ their saviour. Her last words were: 'The Lord is good to all his backsliding children.'

It was then that Frances had told Stephen about her sin. She said she didn't expect to get better because this was God's punishment. And suddenly Stephen realized that that was what he would have said if it had been someone other than Frances, but he just couldn't say it now. He didn't know where his faith had gone. He didn't know what he believed any more.

Anne found it was becoming more than she could cope with. She must talk to Geoff again.

Why Evil and Suffering?

Questions to ponder and discuss

1. Have you ever prayed for someone who was ill? What happened? How did it affect your faith?

2. What is your reaction to Stephen's loss of faith?

3. Consider the way the members of Stephen's church picture God.

5

An Evening with Geoff

Anne hadn't realized how much she had come to depend on Geoff's calm reassurance. He never pushed his own views, but she was sure that underneath there was a very strong and secure faith. He was open to any ideas you threw at him, and always helped you to see a little further, whether it was to put the problem into clearer focus or to open up a fresh way of looking at it.

Together they went over the painful events of recent days. 'Let's try once more to work out where they all stand,' he had said.

'First there's Liz. How do you see her position?' Anne thought for a long time. Geoff didn't press her or break the silence. Then she said, 'I think she took too simple a view of life. She didn't really believe that it would be as difficult as it turned out to be. David had tried to tell her, but she didn't really take it in. When it happened, she just couldn't cope. And because she had trusted in a God who made everything come out right, she lost her faith.'

'How about Stephen, then?' Geoff asked. Again it wasn't easy for Anne. In the end she had to admit that she couldn't understand him. She had disliked his rigid theology so intensely that she had never thought of him as a human being. Now for the first time she saw him as a man who loved his wife passionately. She was his whole life, in fact. 'Stephen's religion was a set of doctrines,' she said, 'but his true life is his love for his wife.' She tried to think out how it was. The thought of losing her made him abandon that theology – it was only superficial, anyway, and it didn't really affect the way he lived, apart from making him censorious of other people. 'I'm glad in a way he has lost his faith,' she said, and then added quickly, 'Isn't that an awful thing to say?'

Why Evil and Suffering?

'Not at all,' Geoff said. 'I think you're probably right. But he needs help.' 'I don't agree at all,' Anne retorted. Geoff looked a little taken aback at her vehemence, then his usual smile came across his face. 'You've taken me wrong,' he said, laughing outright now. 'I didn't mean that we should get him to see a psychiatrist! I meant that he needs our friendship more than he needs any arguments about God. That's all.'

He went on, 'So both Liz and Stephen discovered that the faith which they thought they had crumbled when trouble came to them. It's true they both started from very different positions. As you say, Stephen accepted a set of rigid doctrines. But Liz's faith was much the same. It was just rather pleasanter, that's all. She believed that God would make everything work out right for her. But what about Frances?'

Anne replied straight away this time. 'I can't make her out,' she said. 'She obviously adopted the set of beliefs that Stephen had, but for her they were the absolute basis for her life. Those two were far closer to each other than we ever imagined. Now Stephen has become a human being again and given up all those horrid doctrines, but she has kept them all. Now that she is faced with this dreadful disease she can only say, "I must have sinned, and God is punishing me." Poor thing. She must be in absolute torment. I wonder if she thinks she is going to hell.' Geoff was more solemn than Anne had ever known him. 'I'm afraid she will think just that,' he said very slowly. And then, quite suddenly and with a violence that took Anne completely by surprise; 'What kind of a God do these people think he is? Don't they know what love means? I completely lose patience with them.'

'You know,' Anne said, 'I find myself more and more drawn to David. Just look at the way he is looking after Simon. The only sad thing is that he seems unable to give the same kind of care to Liz.'

And then she went on to talk about Monica. When she had finished Geoff said, 'But that's the easy way out. That's why

An Evening with Geoff

we mustn't take it. We mustn't let go of God quite so readily. There is quite a lot of evidence for his existence, you know. We must talk about that some other time. But what about Fred?'

Again it took Anne a long time before she could put her thoughts together. 'I like him,' she said at last. 'It seems to me that he is perhaps the only true Christian among us all. He has what many people would call a simple faith in Jesus. And yet he isn't stupid. He knows his Bible and loves it in quite a different way from Frances, for whom it seems to be a kind of talisman. He accepts most of what is in the Bible as true, and yet he doesn't let that warp his caring for other people. Did you know that he went to see Frances? He didn't thrust a tract at her, like that woman from Stephen's church did. He simply spoke to her about a great tragedy that had come into his own life and how Jesus had upheld him through it all. I wish I could have a faith like that. But I can't. I see things quite differently.'

'So,' said Geoff, 'that's how you see the five of them. Now the problem for you to work away at is why there are such things as Liz's baby and Frances' cancer in a world which we want to believe God created. You see we also want to believe that he is a God who loves everything he has made far more deeply than we ever love anyone or anything. And the two things just don't match up.'

'Perhaps God simply got caught up in his creation,' said Anne. 'The stuff that he had to work with is just too coarse and rough. He did the best he could.'

'Now there's a thought,' said Geoff. 'We can't start on that trail tonight. It's time I went home. I have to be off early in the morning. I'll be away for about a fortnight.'

Why Evil and Suffering?

Questions to ponder and discuss

1. Does the fact that Stephen lost his faith show that he wasn't a 'real Christian' in the first place?

2. What do you think of Anne's comment: 'I'm glad in a way he has lost his faith'? Why do you think she said it?

3. Think about Liz, Stephen and Frances. What kind of a God did they really believe in? What kind of a God do you believe in?

6

A Further Tragedy

Before Anne could have another talk with Geoff a further tragedy struck the little church community.

Tom was a great old boy. He lived with his wife, who had had a stroke some years before and was now unable to walk and needed to be dressed and put in her wheel chair every morning. Tom looked after her with the utter devotion that sprang from a happy marriage of forty-five years. The nurse came in once a week. Tom was a good cook and his house was smarter than those of many a house-proud woman. He also found time to look after his garden. Before she had had her stroke the garden was his wife's joy and delight. She still liked to be wheeled out on the lawn, where she could watch Tom tend the flowers and vegetables, though he knew she wished she could do the gardening herself. Often he found her in tears. She had never been one to watch other people working. Tom never missed coming to morning service on Sundays. The church was quite near and his wife was safe to be left for an hour in her chair. His cheerful smile was an inspiration to everyone.

They had one son. He had trained as a doctor and was now working in India among the very poorest of the people. When news of the earthquake came Tom was naturally anxious, but he thought that the hospital would be safe. It was. But John had been in the home of an outcaste woman when the earthquake struck and was buried in the rubble. He was dead when they dug him out. Tom's minister had the task of bringing him the sad news.

Everyone in the church rallied round. Tom found their generosity and sympathy almost too much to cope with, especially as all his energies were taken up with comforting his wife. She had been looking forward to her son coming home on holiday in a few months time.

Why Evil and Suffering?

Anne discovered, however, that John's death was dividing the church.

Some of the church members were simply asking why it should have happened to John. He had grown up in the church and had never wavered in his Christian faith. It was because of his commitment to Christ that he had trained to be a doctor and had then gone to help the people he felt needed him most. He was doing a most valuable work among the outcastes and the very poor. He had sacrificed the opportunity of a successful career in this country. So they just asked, 'Why?' without really expecting any answer.

One or two were rather shaken in their faith. They had believed that God would protect his loyal servants from harm – just as the psalmist said: 'A thousand may fall dead beside you . . . but you will not be harmed.' Now that confidence had been undermined. When they asked, 'Why?' it was much more critical. Didn't God care? Was he unable to do anything? Did he even exist? Anne wondered about the kind of faith they had had before. Wasn't it like Liz's? God was a kindly protector who looked after his servants with a special care.

Others retained their unshakeable assurance of God's salvation. 'God has a plan,' they said. 'We don't know what it is, but he does.' Anne was troubled about this. It seemed as if nothing could count as evidence against their belief in God. Whatever happened could be explained ('explained away' was how she put it). If prayers weren't answered it was because you didn't have faith, or you didn't pray hard enough, or God was giving the answer 'No', or he was testing your perseverance. If there was illness or bereavement or any trouble at all, it could be explained as God's way of building up your Christian character.

One of them had described our life on earth as 'a vale of soul-making'. Anne had been rather sharp in her reply. 'What about all the souls who aren't "made"?' she answered. And she thought of Mrs Jones who lived just across the street. She had

A Further Tragedy

lost her husband in a road accident involving a drunken driver soon after they were married. She brought up her son on her own, only to find that he was taking drugs. Then he was convicted of manslaughter after he had killed a man who had tried to prevent him stealing the radio from a neighbour's car. She had looked after her husband's mother for years, even when the old lady became senile and incontinent, refusing to allow her to be taken into care. And suddenly she had snapped, and had never recovered from the nervous breakdown.

Anne had to confess that she found David's reaction more consoling. She had met him on the day after she had heard the news of John's death, and was still feeling rather numb. She had even asked him that same question which so many in the congregation were asking – 'Why did God let it happen?' David had quietly replied, 'I don't think God "let it happen", or could have stopped it, for that matter. There are bound to be earthquakes because that is the way the earth is formed. Where there are rock faults stresses build up and they have to be released in earth movements. We must just learn how to build houses which will withstand earthquakes.' He was silent for a moment as if wondering how Anne was reacting. Then he went on: 'Even if I believed that there is a God, I wouldn't expect him to be able to change geology just to stop a Christian doctor getting killed.' Anne was so surprised and relieved by David's attitude that she asked if he and Liz would come round one evening and they could talk about it a bit more.

Why Evil and Suffering?

Questions to ponder and discuss

1. Can you find an answer to the 'Why?' that the church members were asking?

2. Think about David. John's death wasn't a problem for him: he just accepted the world as it is. Can this be reconciled with the Christian faith?

3. What is meant by saying that the world is 'a vale of soul-making'? Does this provide an answer to the problem of suffering?

7

A Long Talk with Liz and David

It turned out to be a wonderful evening. Liz arranged to have a baby-sitter, and as soon as they came into the room Anne noticed that Liz and David had obviously recovered their old love. She was so pleased that things seemed to be working out for them at last.

They were obviously eager to direct the conversation away from themselves and they soon got talking about John and the earthquake. As well as John so many hundreds of other people had been killed and injured, all of them the very poorest people. 'It doesn't seem fair,' Liz said. 'The rich people can build houses that don't fall down and bury the people in them. It's always the poor who suffer.'

'It isn't a fair world,' David said, adding with half a grin, 'It doesn't pay to be honest.'

So they got to talking about rewards and punishment. Since David didn't believe that there was a God, he found no problems about explaining the unfairness of the world. In his view of the world, evolution means that we have a built-in selfishness. Once it was needed for survival. Now we can't get rid of it, try as we may. So the rich get richer and the poor get poorer. Bad money drives out good, and greed is stronger than altruism.

Liz was sure he was wrong. She felt that the world *ought* to be a place where goodness was rewarded and evil punished. David pointed out that sometimes it did seem to work out like that. He could think of a dozen people who were real saints and whose lives were a joy to themselves and a blessing to everyone they met. There was old Mrs Ashton. She had been the district nurse. How many babies she had brought into the world, before mothers started going into hospital to have their babies. How many people she had laid out with a reverence that you miss today. How often even now she would sit by a sick

Why Evil and Suffering?

person and bring comfort and reassurance into the home. She had a marvellous family of her own, and she and her husband were still sweethearts after fifty-odd years. Life had been good to her, and she would be the first to say that she couldn't doubt God because of the way he had helped her all her life. 'But,' he added, 'I don't believe she has led a charmed life. God has no favourites. It's just chance that it works out like that. And I'm very happy for her. She deserves her good fortune.'

'Odd,' thought Anne, 'that David should say that everything is just a matter of pure chance, and then talk about someone deserving happiness, as if there was somehow someone or something which distributed rewards and punishments.'

But she couldn't get John's death out of her mind. God ought to have protected him. He had given up so much for God and for other people. It was such a waste. And how many more people would suffer now that he wasn't there to help them? It was no good saying that many good people did have a happy life. Many good people didn't. There seemed no sense in the universe at all.

David persisted. 'Would you really want a world where God always rewarded good people and punished those who did wrong? What kind of a world would that really be?' And then he pointed out that although it might seem to be a very comfortable and fair world, in fact it would be quite impossible for there to be any heroic saints. No one would ever be put in the position where they had to say, 'Do what you like to me – torture me, kill me if you want – I will not do this evil thing.'

It was time Liz and David went home. With affectionate hugs they left, and Anne tried to put her thoughts together.

Anne wasn't convinced by what David had said. She honoured men and women like that, but she didn't see that it really helped. After all, John had been killed by an earthquake, not by a tyrant like Hitler. The more she thought about it the less happy she was to pass the blame for all suffering on to evil human beings. It was all very well for David to say that

A Long Talk with Liz and David

evolution made us all selfish, but then he didn't believe in God. If you believed that God had created the universe, then in the end he *was* still responsible for the earthquake – and for evil men and women and the harm they did to other people. And that made him either weak and unable to control the universe he had made, or less than perfectly good. She smiled to herself. Geoff would say she was still thinking she could have contrived things better than God. Was that sinful? At one time Stephen would have said that it was. Frances would still say so. Oh, it was all so difficult!

Questions to ponder and discuss

1. What kind of a world would it be if God always rewarded good people and punished those who did wrong?

2. Try to separate out the suffering caused by human beings and suffering caused by natural disasters, giving examples. What differences can you see between them?

3. Anne thought that she could have contrived things better than God has done. She wondered whether this was sinful. What do you think?

8

Dr Mac

Anne was delighted when the phone rang a couple of days later and she heard a well-loved Scottish voice. Dr MacLaren had been her doctor from when she was a little girl until he retired and moved to his beloved Hebrides. To Anne there never had been a doctor like him – friend, confidant, and doctor all in one. She was even more delighted when he told her that he was staying quite near and asked if he could come over the following day. He came in the middle of the morning.

It was a delightful reunion. They talked over past times. Dr Mac recalled the time Anne had been to Guide camp and came home with an enormous boil on her bottom. And the time she had helped him save old Mr Jackson when he had that heart attack. And that wonderful holiday that she and her brother and younger sister had had with him and his wife at their holiday home on Jura.

Then the talk became more serious. Anne told him about Liz and Simon, about Frances, and John. She knew he was a deeply Christian man. 'Why is there so much suffering in the world?' she asked, 'so much pain?'

'The trouble with you lay people,' he had replied, 'is that you think that suffering and pain are the same things.' He went on to explain that suffering is the opposite of pleasure, but that pain is not the opposite of anything else. It is a purely physical sensation. 'You knew what pain was when you had that boil,' he said with a chuckle.

But Anne said that it didn't make it any better to say that pain was physical. It still hurt. What was the point? Surely God didn't have to create a world where there was pain.

Dr Mac explained that some pain was inevitable. If you have a world of physical bodies and they collide with something hard or sharp they are going to feel pain. It would be much more dangerous for them if they didn't. 'Think,' he said. 'If you dab your hand on the edge of a hot frying pan, you take it off pretty quickly. It's partly a reflex action, of course, but if you didn't feel any pain you might leave it there and get very badly burned.'

Anne saw the point, but she was still not convinced. 'How about my period pains,' she said. 'What good does that misery do me every month?'

'I know, I know,' replied Dr Mac, and he went on to point out that while pain could be a warning of danger, not all pain could be explained that way. He pointed out that if Frances had felt a pain as bad as the worst toothache when the cancer first started in her breast she would have gone straight away to the doctor. Then she could have been completely cured almost for certain. 'It is sad,' he said, 'that many cancers often give no pain at all until they have advanced so far that they are much more difficult to control. Pain doesn't seem to be linked with the seriousness of the disease.' He chuckled. 'Not many people die of toothache.'

He was musing now, and Anne listened, completely fascinated. 'What was the use of the pain of appendicitis to the peasant in the Middle Ages? It was not much good having the warning before we had modern antiseptics and surgery.' He went on to point to other kinds of useless pain, and of the bodies of old women and little children twisted and tortured by disease, and then said quite suddenly, 'Have you read *The Plague* by Camus?'

Anne had, and Dr Mac said that he often felt like Dr Rieux. It was only with great difficulty that he had retained his faith in a loving God. 'Sometimes I have felt that I was working against God. He seems to have invented a universe with so much pain in it, and I was doing my best to set it right. To heal the diseases and to control the pain when I couldn't offer a cure.'

Anne asked what kept his faith alive. 'I'm not sure,' he answered. 'I suppose it was partly my work. When I had my greatest doubts I just threw myself more completely into helping other people and doing all the good that I could. I suppose I'm a bit of an Abou ben Adhem. You know the poem. Abou was not on the list of those whom the angel wrote down as loving God, and asked to be included as one who loved his fellow-men. I hope that like him I shall find that God's love will bless me.'

After Dr Mac had gone Anne found herself thinking again about the vast extent of pain. If some pain is useful, that only meant that the world is rather less evil than we originally thought. We can let God off some of the charges, but a vast amount remains. And is it not made worse by the irrationality of the pain? Some pain is pointless. At other times when we need to feel pain to warn us of disease there is none. And what about the animals?

It was a fresh thought and it kept her awake for several hours before she finally managed to drop off to sleep.

She had no doubt that animals can feel pain, in spite of what some people have said. She remembered how she had shivered on holiday when she was quite a small girl and had heard the cry of a rabbit caught in a snare. That, of course, was human cruelty. But animals do attack each other and prey on one another. Few animals live to old age in the wild.

And what about evolution? That surely must be the greatest challenge to faith. Think of the waste. She tried to remember. Was it only one in a thousand fish eggs that became an adult fish? Was it right that three-quarters of young birds die before they are old enough to breed? Why should these millions and millions of creatures have had to live and suffer and die, just to produce human beings in the end? If that was the purpose of evolution. In that strange way that forgotten quotations suddenly burst into the mind in the middle of the night she remembered how George Bernard Shaw described evolution: 'To modify all things by blindly starving and murdering everything that is not lucky enough to survive in the universal struggle for hogwash.'

Dr Mac

She dreamed about the ichneumon fly, which lays its eggs in the body of a caterpillar. The young grubs start to eat up the living tissues. (In her dream it was like a brood of rats eating through a living sheep.) But the grubs carefully avoided the vital organs that would have killed the caterpillar, and waited until it had turned into a chrysalis before finishing off the job. It was horrible, and when she woke up she could not get to sleep again. Why did God *choose* this way of creating the world, with all its inevitable pain and waste?

She would have to talk to Geoff again as soon as he got back.

Questions to ponder and discuss

1. Would we be better off if we couldn't feel pain?

2. Dr Mac said that sometimes he felt he was working *against* God by trying to heal people and save them from pain. What did he mean by that? Need he have felt this?

3. What would you say to Anne about evolution?

4. Read Albert Camus's *The Plague* (Penguin 1960). What insights has it given you about the problem of suffering? Has it challenged your faith?

9

Geoff has a Get-together with a Few Friends

Geoff was most sympathetic and helpful. He suggested that Anne should join him and two or three friends for a meal and a discussion afterwards.

It turned out that Anne had already met two of the friends, Richard, a university lecturer in Religious Studies and his wife Barbara, who wrote books on spirituality. Geoff had also invited Hilary, one of Richard's colleagues who was in the Biology Department. It was a wonderful meal. Geoff certainly knew how to cook, and Anne soon found that she had no more need to be nervous about Hilary than she had about Richard. They were very down to earth, ordinary people and she enjoyed their company.

Over coffee Geoff opened up the problems as he saw them. If this is God's world and he is a loving God who also possesses perfect and absolute power, why are babies like little Simon born? And why do people like Frances get cancers which are almost certain to kill them unless they're treated in the early stages. He mentioned J. B. Phillips, who lost his faith as a teenager because he saw a dreadful disease turn his witty and vivacious mother into a caricature of a human being. It destroyed her personality and her beauty and left only great weakness and pain. They all knew about the Indian earthquake, and John's tragic death. Anne added what she'd discovered from her day with Dr Mac, and she described her dream.

Geoff looked at Hilary, who said she was pleased that Anne had got her biology right. It was true that there was a great deal of pain in the world of nature, and evolution involves the death of millions of creatures, and only works because they die. But she said that as a biologist she couldn't regard death as evil. 'Look at it this way,' she said. 'To keep the numbers of plants and animals stable, the number of deaths must be equal to the number of births. A world in which no animals died would be a world in which none were born. And that would be a world without courtship, without mating, without bird-song.' She went on to say that she knew that evolution seems pretty horrible, but the surprising thing is that something which appears to be completely blind and haphazard has led to co-operation as well as competition, and in the end produced human beings with values and morals which do not allow the weakest to go to the wall.

Anne was impressed, but not convinced. At the risk of still sounding as if she claimed to be more intelligent and fair-minded than God, she complained that this was all very well, but why should a God who was supposed to be entirely loving and in complete control of everything choose such a cruel method of creating the animals and human beings. Surely he could have avoided all this pain and waste. Why did he make a world in which pain was not only possible but was the fate of everything which had ever lived. She couldn't forget her dream and the grubs of the ichneumon flies. Nor could she get the television pictures of those people in India, crushed beneath their houses or living now as refugees, out of her mind.

Then Richard chipped in. He felt that there was more to be said on God's side! The world had to contain certain regularities or life would be impossible. But this inevitably led to pain and suffering. 'Do you expect a miracle whenever anyone comes into danger? Do you really want water to turn into air every time a little child is nearly drowned? Do you really expect gravity to stop every time someone falls out of a window? That would be a world where there could be no science and it would be impossible to plan anything in advance.'

Anne said that she wasn't wanting miracles like that to happen every moment. She simply thought that God could have devised a world in which there was no pain, or at least far less pain than there was in our world. Richard replied that what she was really wanting was a world that was purely spiritual. 'And why not?' she retorted. 'If our life in heaven is going to be spiritual, why do we have to go through all this misery to get there?'

Barbara sensed that Anne was getting rather het up about it, and she suggested that perhaps it was necessary for us to live in this kind of a world if we were to choose right rather than wrong and to have faith in a God we couldn't see. 'If we are really to be free, perhaps we have to live in our kind of world. Perhaps there was no other way for God.' Anne remembered that man at church who had called the world a 'vale of soul-making'. She had rejected the idea then, and she was no happier with Barbara's suggestion. 'That is too easy a way out,' she said. And she told her about Mrs Jones. 'Is our freedom worth that cost?' she asked.

Geoff had been very quiet throughout this discussion, and everyone was a bit surprised when he spoke. 'I agree with Anne,' he said. And then he pointed to all the great purposeless evils in the world, the kind of evils that they had all met so recently. The earthquake in India that had killed so many Indians as well as Tom's son John. Frances' cancer. Simon, who would never grow into a normal schoolboy. 'At times,' he said, 'I find I just can't believe in God any more. And then I see someone do something that is inexpressibly kind, or I read about someone who has been far braver than I could ever imagine, or I glimpse some quite incredible beauty, and I wonder whether I have been looking on the dark side of things for too long.'

It was getting late and they began to get ready to go home. They had much to think about.

Geoff has a Get-together

Questions to ponder and discuss

1. Anne wanted a world that was completely spiritual. What *is* the point of having to live in a material world before we come to the future life?

2. Anne was unhappy with Barbara's suggestion. Think about the cost of human freedom. Is it worth that cost?

3. Geoff felt that they had forgotten how much goodness and beauty there is in the world. Do you think it is possible to trade off goodness and beauty with suffering in this way?

10

Anne has More to Think About

The next day Anne thought she would go for her favourite walk through the woods and down by the shore. It was a beautiful evening, with the larks singing and a pleasantly cool breeze. Perhaps it would help her to get things straightened out.

To get to the footpath she had to go through the churchyard. There were several paths, but this time she went along one that she had never taken before. Looking idly at the tombstones she suddenly realized that she was passing a row of children's graves. On several of them were some of the toys that they had played with, and very bright and fresh flowers. Anne thought about the parents of these children. How utterly bereft they must feel. And then she noticed one particular stone. It was for a little girl. She read the inscription:

> Jesus wanted an angel,
> someone good and true;
> he looked down from his heaven,
> and, Ann, he took you.

She read it again, and then looked at the dates. Ann was about two and a half years old when she died. Just old enough to be a child who could respond to her parents. Anne had no idea who this other Ann was, but she pictured a smiling little girl, with fair hair and sparkling eyes. Had she been killed in a road accident? Or did some disease strike the cruel blow? Probably it was illness, Anne thought, as she looked again at the stone. Only two and a half years old. And I am alive while she is dead.

She turned away and continued her walk. But those words kept resounding in her head. 'Jesus wanted an angel . . . and, Ann, he took you.' It sounded pious. Probably it gave some comfort to those sorrowing parents. But she didn't believe a

Anne has More to Think About

word of it. She remembered Geoff's angry response to the pious group at church. 'What kind of a God do they think he is?' What kind of a God would kill a tiny child? What suffering had she had to go through before she died? It sounded pious to say that Ann was now an angel with God, but was that what she really believed? Anne wasn't sure. The idea of life after death had always been a problem to her. Yet it wasn't simply that she couldn't be absolutely sure that there was a happy future in heaven for those who had died. It was the thought of Ann and her parents. Their joy when she was born. The happiness of seeing her grow, begin to crawl, speak the first word, run around, going out holding her father's hand. And then – death. Perhaps after much pain. It was bad enough when you asked 'Why,' but to suggest that God had made her ill! To say that Jesus had selfishly taken her because he wanted an angel was the ultimate blasphemy.

As she walked several events in her life came vividly into her mind. There was Wendy. They had been great friends. They sat next to each other in the junior school and vied for being top of the class. Then one day Wendy was away from school. The next Monday the teacher told them all to be very quiet because she had something to tell them that was very sad. Wendy had had diphtheria and had died. Anne's mother had whisked her to the doctor that evening and she had had an injection. She hadn't properly understood how anxious her mother had been. But she was perfectly all right. She hadn't understood it much at the time. Later she kept wondering, 'Why Wendy and not me?'

Then there was Martin. He was the eldest of three children that Anne sometimes played with. He too had died. Not long after, their two mothers met in the street and talked about his death. Anne didn't remember much about what they said except for one sentence that Martin's mother had spoken very quietly: 'He seemed ready to go.'

Why Evil and Suffering?

A few years ago there had been another young person who had died. Felicity was the daughter of one of the keenest members of her church. She had been diagnosed as having leukaemia, but in someone quite young there was a good hope of recovery. The church members had prayed. Then one day the steward ended the reading of the notices with: 'The latest news we have is that Felicity is quietly slipping away.' Anne had questioned it at the time. Why were their prayers not heard? Why had someone so young been allowed to die? And again there were some in the church who said, 'God has taken her to himself,' and others who quoted those lines from the hymn that Anne now found to be so irritating: 'God moves in a mysterious way.'

Once again Anne found herself much more at home with David, who simply accepted it as part of life. Without any God to have to try to understand and excuse, it was so much easier. And yet . . . 'There must be a God,' she found herself saying out loud. And then looked round anxiously in case anyone had heard her. Fortunately no one was there.

She had reached the end of her walk now and turned back for home. When she came to the gravestone she looked at it again. 'I can't believe that,' she said to herself. 'I won't. It may have comforted little Ann's parents, but it just won't do for me. I simply do not believe that God treats us just like a child playing with dolls. I can't think of God as someone who causes illness. If that were true then doctors and nurses are all fighting God, as Dr Mac said.' It was such an outrageous idea that she stopped walking. 'I suppose it's all a matter of what kind of a world we think it is.' That at least was something slightly less painful to think about, and she soon reached home.

She wondered about ringing Geoff, but decided against it. He must be getting tired of her constant questions and pestering. She would just have to try to work it out for herself.

Anne has More to Think About

Questions to ponder and discuss

1. The death of small children troubles us all. What would you say to a parent whose child had died?

2. What is your reaction to that tombstone?

3. Felicity died even though many people were praying for her. What explanation would you give to someone who had stopped praying because this had happened?

11

Not in Our Little Town!

Everyone knew old Mr Grant. He had lived all his life in the house in which he had been born. He had worked in the town until he retired. Now he was a very sprightly eighty-seven, and lived on his own in his beautifully cared-for house and garden. He was never ill. Whenever you met him in the street he would give a cheery 'Good morning!' 'Good afternoon!' Never 'Hello!' That wasn't his style. And he was always the same. When everyone else was grumbling about the rain, or the cold, or the gas company, or the government, Mr Grant would find something good to say about them. And if anyone needed any help he would be there to give it, whether it was sitting with someone who was ill, or getting the groceries for someone who couldn't get out. Somehow he always seemed to know when anyone needed help, and he was there. Everyone knew him as George – but they didn't call him that to his face. He liked to be called 'Mr Grant'.

Now he was dead. The police had been called to his house by the paper boy, who found the door wrenched open. It was all round the town. The old man had been brutally beaten and stabbed many times. His house was wrecked.

Whenever people met in the street they spoke with subdued voices. 'You wouldn't expect it here – not in our little town' was said over and over again. They reminded each other of Mr Grant's goodness. 'He wouldn't hurt a fly,' was how many of them expressed it. 'He was the kindest man you would ever meet.' Others said that if everyone was like George the world would be a much better place. Most of all what they were all asking was, 'Why pick on George?'

He wasn't a churchman – 'If I get to heaven,' he used to say, 'I will hold out my hands to God and say to him, "Look at my hands".' But they remembered him at Anne's church the next Sunday, and prayed for his family. At the end of the service no one was eager to leave. They talked quietly. Again and again the same question was asked: 'Why pick on George?' But Anne sensed that they were beginning to give different answers.

On Thursday Anne happened to meet Barbara in the library. She found herself saying, 'Is our freedom worth that?' Barbara tried to explain that freedom is all or nothing. If people are to be free to choose goodness, they have to be free to choose evil – and some of them will. This wasn't good enough for Anne. 'Surely,' she argued, 'it must have been possible for God to create people who were free, but who would never deliberately choose evil.' She thought of George. If ever there was a man who was free, he was. You sensed his freedom every time you were with him. And yet as everyone kept on saying since his death, 'You always knew exactly what he would do. He was always the same.' She recalled how his brother had once said to her: 'George never put on a show for strangers. He was just the same at home: quiet, patient, cheerful, caring, thoughtful.' 'Why couldn't God have made everyone like that?' Anne asked.

While she was speaking Alistair came into the library, and when he saw the two of them talking he joined them. Anne didn't know Alistair very well. He was a member of the church that Stephen had joined. 'Now do you believe in original sin?' he said. Anne was shocked that he seemed to put doctrine before a human concern for George. What must it have been like to be beaten to death? How terrified the old man must have been! How he must have suffered! Alistair didn't seem to notice, and went on with his harangue about the government being soft with criminals, and all these trendies who didn't believe in evil. 'Teachers aren't strict enough,' he said, and went on at length about the failure of everyone nowadays to accept the Fall. 'Even church leaders don't believe in the Devil or hell any more.'

At last he stopped, and Barbara quietly said, 'I believe in original sin, even though I don't believe that there was a

Why Evil and Suffering?

historical Fall.' Alistair was just about to quote some verses from Paul, but Barbara went on: 'All of us, if we are honest, know that we are always likely to do things that we know are wrong. And all of us know just as clearly that there are many things which we ought to have done to help other people, and we didn't do them because we were too lazy or wanted to spend the time doing something else for ourselves.'

Alistair wasn't convinced that she was a 'true believer', as he put it, but he was glad that someone was prepared to face up to human nature as it really was. After he had gone to choose his books, Barbara and Anne talked a little longer. Then they parted, and Anne checked out her books at the counter and went home.

On reflection, she found the conversation puzzling. She could understand Alistair's position, even though she disagreed with it profoundly. But Barbara's attitude seemed inconsistent. If she simply meant that nearly everyone found it easier to choose evil rather than good, fair enough. But then, why call it 'original sin'? For didn't that phrase really involve accepting an original innocence that had been lost? She just didn't believe that there had ever been an age of innocence.

But then she tried to think back to what Barbara had said at Geoff's get-together. She had explained much of the suffering in the world by saying that it was the result of human beings doing evil things, and that was the price we had to pay for freedom. 'So George's mangled body is the price of my freedom to choose between right and wrong,' she muttered. 'Well, I am not prepared to accept the price.' And then after a pause, 'I wonder what David would say.'

Not in Our Little Town!

Questions to ponder and discuss

1. Do you think that it is possible for God to create human beings who are truly free and yet never do evil?

2. Both Barbara and Alistair used the term 'original sin'. Try to think out the differences between what they each meant by it. Do you believe in either of these ideas?

3. If you were David or Fred, what would you say about George's murder.

12

An Evening with Geoff, David, and Fred

As it happened Anne soon had a chance to find out. Liz invited her round the next evening. She told her that David had been extremely distressed about George's murder and wanted to talk to someone about it. Geoff was coming as well, and she had asked Fred to join them.

When she arrived she found the other two were already there and Liz had just gone out. David was indeed very upset. It seemed to him that society was breaking down. If people could do that to a harmless old man like George, would Simon ever be safe out of their sight? And what would happen to Simon when he and Liz were no longer there to look after him? It seemed that while he was prepared to accept that disasters like the earthquake and children born with Down's syndrome were a part of the natural order, he found it impossible to cope with senseless cruelty by human beings.

Anne told him what Barbara had said, but this wasn't enough for David. Like Anne, he was unwilling to take what he regarded as the easy way out by saying that this was the inevitable price of freedom. 'If that is the price, I am not prepared to pay it,' he declared.

Geoff suggested that they should look at it in the same way as they accepted Simon. It was all part of the evolutionary process. Selfishness was built into human nature because of the way the human race had evolved. But this was still not good enough for David. With his mind he accepted that it was so, but he reacted so strongly against the barbaric attack on George that he was morally revolted. After Simon had been born it almost looked as if he would come to accept some kind of a belief in God, but now he rejected the idea completely. 'How can there be a God who is loving and caring, and at the same time is completely in control of the whole universe, who would allow such monsters as George's murderers to appear in his

An Evening with Geoff, David, and Fred

world.' He was outraged at the idea. 'If God knows everything,' he said, 'and if he is all-powerful, then he is responsible for George's murder. You cannot find any excuses for him. He is a fiend, not a father.'

Anne was shaken. David had seemed so level-headed, so 'normal'. She had wished several times that she could be like him, taking life as it came and doing his best to make it better. But now he seemed to have lost all of his old confidence. Deep inside herself she realized that he was expressing many of the doubts that she herself had. Yet she felt that David really wanted to believe in God, just as she did. If he hadn't, he wouldn't have been so vehement in his attack on God. She looked at Fred.

Fred didn't speak immediately. After some minutes (to Anne the silence seemed to last for hours), he said, very quietly, 'I think we are right to be rebellious and angry. I don't believe that God would wish us to react in any other way.'

Anne was so surprised that she didn't know what to say. This was a side of Fred that she didn't know existed. David too was silent. Fred went on. 'I think we have something to learn from the psalmists and from Job. They were quite prepared to question God, to shout at him, almost to curse him to his face. And the marvellous thing is that God seemed almost pleased that they did so. You see, I don't believe that God expects us to be always grovelling before him and telling him that his will is best.' He uncrossed his legs and crossed them again. 'You know, if there is one thing that I just cannot accept it is when people say, "God moves in a mysterious way" when something quite dreadful has happened. How I hate these platitudes! "It's all for the best!" I just don't believe that that is what Jesus would have said. The Lord Jesus would have offered comfort first. Then he would have spoken about his Father's love.' They were silent. After a while, Fred added, 'I wish I knew my heavenly Father as well as Jesus knew him.'

Why Evil and Suffering?

For the first time that evening David looked relieved. 'So you don't think I'm beyond the pale, then?' he said, with what was almost a smile. 'Not at all,' said Fred. 'I think you have reacted to that attack on George in the only way a sensitive human being could.' His sudden silence made Anne wonder whether he had intended to say more but thought better of it. 'Perhaps,' she mused, 'he was going to say that David was on the way to discovering Jesus for himself.'

At that moment Liz came back. She sensed immediately that David was much calmer than he had been during the last few days. He looked up at her and their eyes met. 'Shall we tell them?' she said. David nodded, and Liz said, 'We're going to have another baby.' After the others had congratulated them, David said, 'It really was so important that the three of you came round this evening. You see I had been saying that this wasn't the kind of world to bring another child into. We almost started to have that dreadful quarrel about abortion again. I am still not quite sure, but you have given me a little more confidence. I must read the Gospels and the book of Job.'

Questions to ponder and discuss

1. David found human cruelty more difficult to accept than material disasters. Consider whether it is a greater problem for Christians.

2. David said that, if there is a God, he is responsible for George's murder. What do you think?

3. God is greater than all our thoughts. Why then did Fred reject the line from the hymn, 'God moves in a mysterious way'?

4. Geoff said very little. What do you suppose he may have been thinking?

13

Anne and David Turn to the Bible

So Anne read the book of Job. She remembered that, when she had been worried about the meaning of the Bible, the book of Job had opened her eyes to its value. The story of the man who had lost everything seemed to fit in exactly with the doubts that she and her friends were facing.

It was the first time David had read it, and he found it very difficult. Anne had been so enthusiastic about it that he had expected it to explain why there is so much suffering in the world. He had been looking for a clear argument, but it seemed to him more like four deaf people talking to each other. Bits of it were very beautiful, but he couldn't understand most of it. Even the story at the beginning and end seemed just to say that, if you held on, everything would work out all right in the end. And he just didn't believe that. He decided that he would have to get Geoff and Anne to come round and explain what it all meant.

In fact they met at Geoff's, because Geoff said that they really needed to have an expert, and he would see if Richard could join them. Geoff got Richard to start them off. 'It is a book from long ago,' he explained. 'People looked at things rather differently from the way we do. We mustn't expect to find a philosophical debate in the book. Rather the writer is saying, "If you want to see what suffering is like, look at this one man Job." Perhaps the most important thing that we can learn from the book is the different reactions to suffering by Job and the friends. Job's relations with God are the most important of all.' And he suggested that they should look at some bits of the book together.

They read them aloud. 'We all know the story,' said Richard, 'so we'll start with chapter 3.' So they read about Job's utter despair. 'That's a bit like I felt,' said David. They then turned to 7.17–20. 'It's a bitter parody of Ps. 8,' Richard explained,

Why Evil and Suffering?

and they turned up that psalm and compared it with what Job said. 'Job had a very warped picture of God,' said Anne, when they read his account of God as a cruel torturer in 16.7–14. 'But look at 23.3–9,' said Richard. 'Even if he thinks that God is such a fiend, he still longs to meet him.' Last of all they read chapters 29–31. 'I like that,' said Anne. 'It seems to sum up the whole book. Job is describing his happiness when he was prosperous, and then tells us about his sufferings. But last of all he claims that he is perfectly good. I think of him striding into God's presence like a prince, and demanding to know the charge that God has against him. It's as if he is saying: "Show me my indictment. You'll find it is an acquittal that I shall be proud to wear as a crown."'

'But what about those speeches by God?' David said. 'If I had been Job, I shouldn't have been satisfied to be told to look at a hippopotamus! I don't think the book has any answer to our problems at all.'

Richard explained that in Old Testament times people could only think of God as the majestic and all-powerful One. 'We must remember that the writer of the story of Job lived before Jesus came. We can't expect him to picture God as we do, now that we have seen Jesus. The important thing is that Job had met God. That was what satisfied him. He realized at last that no one could stride into God's presence like a prince once they had seen him in all his holiness.'

Geoff added that every time he read the book of Job he found something new in it that helped him with his faith. It was his favourite book in the whole Bible.

But Anne was worried. It seemed to her that up till now they had all been talking like philosophers. They were trying to find an explanation for the things that had happened: why Simon had Down's syndrome, why Frances had cancer, why God had allowed John to die in the earthquake, and why God had created human beings who were so evil that they would attack old Mr Grant like that. Even when they read the book of Job

Anne and David Turn to the Bible

they were still talking about problems and answers. Where did Jesus come in? Surely, if they were to understand God, they must look at the New Testament. 'I wish Fred were here,' she said. 'I would like to know what he would say.'

Geoff wasn't too sure about it all. He was afraid that if they simply talked about Jesus that might make it just a bit too easy. 'Think of those friends of Stephen's who are now saying that he is a back-slider. They are all too ready to say that all the evil in the world is due to the Fall. Then they preach to us that we must trust in Jesus as our personal saviour and find salvation in the blood of the cross. It's as if they are only interested in plucking us out of the wicked world and sending us to heaven. If you express any doubts, you aren't a "real Christian". I have no patience with them.'

Richard obviously had considerable sympathy with Geoff, but he agreed with Anne that as Christians they must look for answers in the New Testament. 'In the first place,' he said, 'listen to Paul. He had a serious illness of some kind that he calls "a stake in the flesh", and he tells us that he prayed to God three times and asked him to take it away. But God's answer was, "My grace is all you need, for my power is greatest when you are weak"' (II Cor. 12.7–9).

Anne wasn't satisfied. 'Paul sounds just like those people who always has an explanation for any prayer that isn't answered,' she said. But Geoff suggested that it all depended on your attitude. It might not be the answer to *our* questions, but it was an answer for Paul and it might be the answer for Frances.

'But what about Jesus?' Anne asked. 'I know he was fully human so that we must interpret everything he said and did in the light of first-century Palestine where he lived, but surely we ought to pay attention to him.'

Geoff said that he always felt that the most important thing about Jesus was that he was totally opposed to suffering. That meant that it was never right to say that God *sent* suffering, or

Why Evil and Suffering?

that God punished us by making us suffer. 'So Dr Mac needn't have felt that he was working against God,' said Anne. 'That's right,' Geoff replied. 'Everyone who tries to heal disease and prevent suffering is on God's side.'

It was David who spoke last before they broke up and went home. 'I don't think there are any answers,' he said. And then, after a pause, he added, 'And I still don't think I understand the book of Job. But I have learnt one thing from that book. If there is a God – and I just don't know whether I believe he exists or not – but if there is a God, then I must be absolutely honest with him and not try to hide my doubts and my anger. And if Jesus really was God's way of coming to us, God must be a wounded God. I am sure that that is the only kind of God who can help me.'

Questions to ponder and discuss

1. Read the passages from the book of Job that the friends read. In what ways are they a help in thinking about the problem of suffering?

2. Anne wished that Fred had been there. What do you think Fred might have said if he had been?

3. Why do you think that Geoff was so hard on Stephen's friends?

4. Try to think out what David meant by 'a wounded God'.

Part 2

Thinking Through the Issues

14

Sorting out the Problem

One of the things which our story has shown is that we are all very mixed up in our thinking about suffering, and perhaps the first thing we need to do is to try to sort this out.

Pain and Suffering

We can start with Dr Mac. He pointed out the important difference between pain and suffering. We often think of them as exactly the same. Yet, as he showed, strictly pain is purely physical. There is evidence that there are specific pain-receptor nerves which are triggered off either by direct impact (as when someone sticks a pin in us) or by the production of chemicals in the cells surrounding the pain nerve. Aspirin and paracetamol work by inhibiting the production of these chemicals and so reduce the ache.

Pain usually causes suffering. But pain isn't the only cause. Some of our worst suffering is mental. Those who have suffered the anguish of bereavement know this, and the rest of us can probably recall something which made us suffer, although it wasn't physical pain.

Natural Evils and Moral Evil

Then we need to distinguish between different kinds of evil. The most obvious difference is between physical or natural evil and moral evil. The cancer from which Frances suffered and the Indian earthquake that killed John and all the other people are natural evils. Other natural evils are such things as flood, volcanic eruptions, drought, and the many kinds of disease. On the other hand, George's murder was a moral evil, and we can readily think of a vast range of similar evils of different levels of seriousness, from lying and theft to rape and torture.

Why Evil and Suffering?

We can make the difference clear by saying that moral evil is evil that human beings produce, while natural evil is the evil that we find in the world itself, independently of human beings. Normally we think of natural evils as evil only when they affect human beings. Perhaps we ought to include animals. When the next-door cat kills the greenfinch that we have been feeding in our garden is that evil? Or we can ask: Are the destruction and waste that seem to be an inevitable part of evolution evils?

Natural evil and moral evil are often linked, of course. Famine in Africa is a natural disaster caused by drought, but the suffering it produces has been greatly increased by the moral evils of war. And if the rich countries supply the weapons that fuel that war, or give too little help to those who are dying of starvation, these moral evils increase the suffering that the drought sparked off. In general terms, much suffering that is the result of poverty and illness has been made worse because vast sums of money are spent on armaments and space research, instead of on caring for the poor and paying for hospitals, doctors and nurses. Wrong priorities in the creation and use of wealth are moral evils that increase suffering, even if they don't originally cause it. One writer has even claimed that modern capitalism itself has killed more children than were destroyed in Hitler's death camps, though many would regard this as a political statement rather than a philosophical or theological one.

Only One God

While we are trying to get our initial ideas straight, we should also look at our ideas of God. In Christian tradition there is only one God. This means that we cannot, *as Christians*, explain the evil in the world by attributing it to a malign god who fights against the good one. But we shouldn't reject this belief entirely out of hand as we discuss the problem of evil. If we are going to be honest in our search for truth, we must look

Sorting out the Problem

carefully at every main proposal that human beings have put forward. But one reason why evil was such a serious problem for the people of the Old Testament is that they believed that there was only one God. He created everything. This meant that drought, earthquake, flood, famine, and disease were all caused directly by him. And when the Psalmist was ill and prayed to God, he sometimes complained that God must be asleep because he did nothing to help him.

Omnipotence and Omniscience

Christians believe that God is all-powerful. He must also be all-knowing, since it would be of little use to be able to do anything he chose if he didn't know what the consequences of his actions might be.

These aren't easy ideas to deal with.

The joke question is 'Can God create a stone too heavy for him to lift?' Philosophers have found considerable scope for discussion about this, but for most of us the question points to one important fact about omnipotence. God cannot do things that break the rules of logic. This means that he cannot create a square circle or a triangle with four corners. We shall see the importance of this when we pick up Anne's suggestion that God could have made people who were free but never committed sin.

Omniscience is equally difficult for us to comprehend. We might think that, if God is really God, he must know everything. There is no difficulty in thinking of him knowing everything that is happening anywhere in the universe at this particular moment. But does omniscience mean that he knows what you are going to do next Wednesday evening? We cannot go into the intricacies of time and the future here. It is enough to suggest that our free-will may be one of the things which limit both God's power and his knowledge. Of course ultimately he chose to give us free-will, and so if this limits him in any way, it was his own decision. But we shall have to think later on about how 'free' our free-will actually is.

Good and Evil

Things are a little more difficult if we ask whether God could treat torture as a good deed. Here again philosophers have had long discussions about whether there is a standard of goodness against which God's own actions can be judged. One answer is to say that God is limited by his character, and cannot command anything which is contrary to his own goodness.

There is a little more to be said about this, however. You will remember that Anne was horrified when Stephen said that God's ways weren't our ways and we couldn't understand his purposes. Here too philosophers find difficulties that many of us are happy to overlook, but the main point must be that, even though we cannot know or understand God's ultimate will, any further discussion about the problem of evil becomes impossible unless his idea of goodness is closely similar to ours. As Anne pointed out, if we admit that God's idea of goodness may be different from ours, this might mean that what we regard as evil might be good to him.

This has an important consequence. It means that nothing which we, in our best moments, believe to be wrong can ever be right for God. We cannot make God less moral than we are.

Two Errors

So although we must recognize that God is far greater than we can ever think or imagine, we must accept that his character is supreme goodness and that his goodness is similar to what we regard as good. But there is still a little more to be said.

We must be careful to avoid two false views of God. On the one hand we don't know God's mind. That was the chief error of Job's friends. They thought that they knew exactly how God

Sorting out the Problem

ruled the world, and when Job didn't fit into their tidy scheme of things, they decided that he must be a great sinner. They even 'rewrote' his life to make it fit their doctrine of God. It was also the error of Stephen's friends, when they said that Stephen and Frances lacked faith and that, if they had truly believed, Frances would have been healed. A great Christian mystic made the point in a memorable sentence. He said, 'A God who is completely known is not a God at all.'

The other error is to use the mystery of God to enable us to wriggle out of any difficulty. This was the mistake of those who thought that it was pious to repeat the familiar lines from the hymn, 'God moves in a mysterious way / His wonders to perform.' Anne was quite right in being unwilling to let God off the hook in this way. We possess minds and ought not to adopt a religion which forces us to stop thinking. The evils that we meet raise a real problem which has to be faced and thought through. It isn't a sign of great faith to refuse to accept that the problem exists.

So when we are thinking about God, we need to remember that he is far greater than our highest thoughts and that even the most saintly and wise men and women can never comprehend his mind. But we also need to be careful that we don't use our ignorance to explain every problem that meets us.

Our Aim

One last point. We need to be clear about what we are trying to do. In their different ways all the actors in our story were trying to face up to things which they regarded as evil. Most of them wanted to retain their belief in God, although David was an agnostic and Stephen lost his faith because he was crushed by the cancer which attacked Frances. Anne, Geoff, Fred, Richard, and Barbara saw that there was a contradiction between their belief in a God who is a loving Father and the pain and suffering which they or their friends or relatives had to endure.

Why Evil and Suffering?

Even Liz, who responded emotionally rather than rationally, wanted to trust in a God who was kind and helpful. Often we all fail to notice contradictions between what we say we believe and how we react to what happens around us. We simply couldn't cope with being absolutely logical all the time. But when the tension is too great, we have to find some explanation. In our story everyone made some attempt to do that. In one way or another they asked the question, 'Why does God allow evil?' What we are going to do now is to examine some of the answers they gave and try to discover whether these answers are valid.

Questions to ponder and discuss

1. Collect up some more examples of natural and moral evils. Does it help to treat them separately?

2. What picture of God do you have? (Think about some of the terms like 'all-powerful', 'omniscient/all-knowing', that have been used in this chapter to describe him.)

3. In several places in the Bible God is said to be different from human beings (Num. 23.19; I Sam. 15.29; 16.7). In what ways is he different? Does this mean that his ideas of goodness are different from ours?

15

Some Dead Ends

Evil as Unreal

All of our characters accepted that evil is real. There have been some people, however, who have argued that illness and other kinds of evil are imaginary. You may have met members of the Christian Scientist Church, who follow the teachings of Mrs Baker Eddy. She declared that evil is simply an illusion and doesn't really exist. Evil is false belief, and if sin, sickness, and death were rightly understood as nothingness, they would disappear. To most of us this seems to be absurd, and since this isn't a book about Christian Science, we will leave the matter there.

Evil as the Absence of Good

There is a more reputable suggestion, however, to which we ought to pay a little attention, though we shall dismiss it almost as quickly. This is the idea that evil is not positive and powerful in itself but is rather a falling away from the goodness which God intended his creatures to have. In other words, evil is the absence of goodness rather than something real in itself. We can sympathize with the motive behind this idea. It was put forward in order to avoid the idea that God created evil. So it is argued that everything which God created was good, and evil is simply the failure of his creatures to live as he intended. The difficulty with this is that we experience evil as very much a real fact. To suggest that torture is the absence of caring love seems to many of us to be as absurd as to say that the pain which the victim feels is unreal. We could say much more about this, but it will be sufficient for our argument to accept the common-sense view of evil as something which exists in our world and has to be explained.

Why Evil and Suffering?

Intractable Matter

The next point will take us a little longer. You will remember that Anne suggested to Geoff that perhaps God had simply got caught up in his creation. 'The stuff that he had to work with is just too coarse and rough. He did the best he could' (p. 21). This is an idea which goes back as far as Plato, and is still with us today in different forms. We might offer it a double knock-out blow by saying that it contradicts our conception of God as all-powerful, and it makes matter eternal alongside of God and so conflicts with our idea of God as the creator of everything that exists. But we ought not to be quite so hasty.

As long as we accept evolution as the method by which God created his universe, we have to face a number of questions. Perhaps God just started it off and then left it to run its own course. On the other hand, perhaps he has been directing every stage of its progress. Did he limit himself when he chose to create the universe through its evolution? What part does chance play in it all? These are all important – and difficult – questions.

The picture of a God who just started it all off has an honourable pedigree, but it would remove God completely from our present experience. It would mean that there is little difference between this God who was there only at the moment of the 'big bang' at the beginning of it all and the idea that the material universe just exists, without anyone having created it, curious though we may think that idea to be. We must all wonder at some time why the world is here, and not just nothing – but that is another problem, and another book!

But we cannot go to the other extreme and think of God as controlling every moment of the development of the universe, because our scientific understanding of evolution is that it proceeds though natural processes that do not require constant interference by an outside being. Most scientists feel very uneasy about suggesting that God somehow directed evolution so that it led to the appearance of human beings. While Darwin's own theory of natural selection has been modified, no biologist would deny that evolution has taken place and that it can be explained by scientific 'laws', even if we are a long way from discovering them all.

To make sense of the way God might work through evolution is exceedingly difficult, and various pictures and analogies have been suggested. We might think of God, for example, as a great chess player, who works within the rules of the game and counters the moves of his opponent to obtain a checkmate. He is limited by the physical 'laws' that he has created, but is able to work his purposes by 'using' them. Or we might suggest that part of the perfection of God is that he possesses the power to develop along with his creation. Many people would say that that makes God less than 'perfect', but it has been put forward by serious Christian thinkers. These are all intriguing suggestions, but we cannot follow them up here. It will be enough simply to accept that both evolution and human free-will appear to impose limitations upon God's power, but that this doesn't make him less than God. Indeed, the fact that he has *voluntarily* chosen to limit himself in these ways may point to his greater goodness.

An Evil God alongside the Good God

There is one last dead end that we need to block off before we can begin our search for an answer to our question about evil. Some people have pictured the world as a battle ground between two opposing gods, one good and one evil. It is known as 'dualism'. We saw that this is ruled out by the Christian belief in only one God who is the creator of everything. To adopt dualism as a solution of the problem of evil, therefore, involves abandoning Christianity. The tough-minded will say that this is no absolute denial of its truth, and we should be prepared to reject Christianity if it were shown to be false. It

Why Evil and Suffering?

certainly provides a completely adequate reason for the presence of evil in our world, but it does so at considerable cost. If there are two equal gods, how can we be sure that the good one will win in the end? Perhaps he will be defeated by the evil god. Or at a more logical and religious level, what motive would there be for siding with the good god? If both are equal, there is no reason why we should choose the good one, apart from our sense that goodness is better than evil. In practice, of course, all those who believe in two opposing gods are confident that the good one will triumph in the end. So the dualism of two opposing gods hasn't appealed to many people.

The main religion which accepts the idea of two opposing gods is Zoroastrianism. Its adherents believe that there are two personified forces in the universe. Ahura Mazda is the source of all that is good, including success, health and immortality. Opposite him is Ahriman, the source of all that is evil – misfortune, disaster, war, sickness, and death. Our world is the great battlefield between Ahura Mazda and Ahriman, and human beings must choose between them. But Ahriman is never the equal of Ahura Mazda, because he cannot foresee what Ahura Mazda is going to do. He can only react against him, and in the end he is doomed to defeat.

Belief in the devil can perhaps be seen as a version of dualism. The difference is that while dualism accepts the existence of two equal and eternal Gods, the devil is a fallen 'angel' who was created by God. The idea has a firm place within Christian tradition, although it isn't as central as many people suppose. Our picture of Satan has tended to be influenced more by Milton than by the Bible, though probably few people today read *Paradise Lost*.

Ideas of a demonic opponent of God came into Jewish thought very late in the history of ancient Israel. 'The satan' (not yet a proper name) in Job and Zechariah is a member of God's heavenly court, and while he may appear to be rather cynical, his job is to test the goodness and faith of men and

Some Dead Ends

women, and that seems to be legitimate in principle. It is only in the late book of Chronicles that Satan has become a personal name, and there he 'tempts' David to conduct a census for which David is then punished by God. (The references are Job 1.6–12; 2.1–8; Zechariah 3.1–2; I Chronicles 21.1. The last is a different version of II Samuel 24.1.)

By the time of Jesus ideas of demons had been accepted by many Jews, and in this respect Jesus was no different from the people among whom he lived. It was even believed that there was a hierarchy of them under a leader who had various names of which Satan was only one. The view which many Christians down the years have held is that the evil in the world is caused by fallen angels, and especially by the devil. It has been linked with the story of Adam and Eve in Genesis 3, which was taken to be historical. According to this theology, evil came into the word as the result of the Fall. Christians have also uttered warnings against being tempted by the devil. We shall look at the idea of the Fall in the next chapter.

Even though Jesus certainly believed in the existence of Satan or Beelzebub, there is no reason for us to do so. He belonged to his own age and accepted the ideas of his contemporaries. There are three objections to attributing all evil and suffering to the devil.

First, ideas of Satan and demons came into Judaism very late, – perhaps from Zoroastrianism. We may, therefore, decide that such a belief isn't central to the Bible, although this does not necessarily mean that it isn't true.

Second, the idea of a 'fallen angel' is particularly suspect. Angels (if they exist) would know God in all his full goodness and splendour, and while they do not possess all knowledge, their understanding must be far greater than any human intelligence. It is difficult, therefore, to understand why any of them should 'fall'.

Thirdly, any power which the devil might possess would have been granted to him by God. As an explanation of evil and

Why Evil and Suffering?

suffering which exonerates God, therefore, it fails. God would still be ultimately responsible for all the evils that occur in the world.

No form of dualism provides an answer to our problem

Questions to ponder and discuss

1. Have you known any Christian Scientists? If you have, what do they say about suffering? What do you make of their ideas?

2. Think about some of the crimes that you have heard about recently – reported on the radio or television or in the paper. Why isn't it satisfactory to think of evil as the absence of good?

3. Anne was attracted to the idea that God simply did the best he could with coarse and rough matter. Why is this unsatisfactory as an explanation of the evil in the world?

4. Many people say that the evil in the world is due to the devil. What do you think about this explanation?

16

Two False Trails

Anne was desperately worried by the ideas of the extremely conservative Christians ('Stephen's friends'), and we need to look at these first.

Suffering as Punishment

A very common idea, among those people who wouldn't call themselves religious as well as with church members, is that suffering is punishment. They believe something like this. The world is a testing ground. God rewards those who obey him and punishes those who don't. 'Stephen's friends' would express it in more religious language, and say that God looks after those who have accepted Jesus as their personal saviour and believe in the cross for salvation. In its more grotesque forms it is the message of the American television evangelists who promise riches and health to true believers. 'Stephen's friends' wouldn't express their ideas as crudely as this, but their beliefs are somewhat similar.

It is an idea which appeals to our sense of fairness. The daughter of a man who had a fatal heart attack on the bus as he was going home from his last day at work described it as 'so unfair' that he couldn't enjoy a happy retirement. Ministers know how often a sick person will ask, 'What have I done to deserve this?' And it lies behind the reaction to John's death in the earthquake. He had trained to be a doctor and was helping extremely poor and needy people. Why did God allow him to die? This sense of unfairness also lies behind Anne's reaction to the death of the small children and her memory of the three people who died from illnesses. We all think that goodness ought to be rewarded and evil punished.

Probably there aren't very many people who are like Job's friends and argue that because someone suffers then they must

Why Evil and Suffering?

have committed some great sin. But there are more who are like Frances. The sudden onset of illness, either in themselves or in their loved-ones, makes them look back on their lives and accuse themselves of some wrongdoing which can account for the suffering, and they then become wracked with guilt. This in itself may hinder their healing, and always it damages their relations with their loved-ones and their friends. It is important, therefore, that this idea be firmly rejected.

There are several ways to attack it.

First, we might ask how we think it actually is supposed to work out. Is the idea that God personally intervenes and bashes the wicked person? Simply to express the thought in this way is probably enough to show us how unacceptable it is. It would mean that God deliberately inflicts pain on people who have committed some wrong, and that is plainly neither true nor moral. Even on a human level we are constantly being forced to question the ways we treat criminals, and the picture of God as a kind of superior gaoler or executioner, someone who inflicts physical punishment on people who do wrong, is below our own highest ideals. Retribution isn't the highest motive for punishment. Sometimes it is positively evil.

Secondly, many writers in the Old Testament deny that prosperity and illness exactly match the character and deeds of men and women. It just doesn't work out that way. If we look about us we can think of people we know who prove this. There are good men (like Mr Grant in our story) who suffer greatly, while we probably know of cheerful rogues who always seem to get away with it.

Moreover, as the book of Job shows, if everything did work out neatly like that, and goodness was always rewarded, we should be living in Satan's world and not God's. It would be a world in which doing good was a way to certain success. And the supreme goodness of following our conscience in face of the worst that men or women could do to us would be impossible. A world in which God always protected those who believe in him or live good lives wouldn't be a *moral* world at all.

In the third place, we must assure those who are suffering that their illness and pain aren't punishment for any wrongs that they have done. This is part of the comfort which they need and we should give it rather than increase their suffering by telling them that if they truly believed they would have healing. Remember Frances. She believed that her cancer was God's punishment for her early indiscretion. Worse, she believed that she was a sinner and probably would go to hell. Do we really think that that would be just?

It is true that goodness and happiness frequently go together, and wrongdoing often leads to suffering, if not in the wicked person, at least for those they affect (we might think of the child killed by a driver who was over the limit). But the suggestion, which some have made, that AIDS is divine punishment for homosexual practices, is blatantly false and needs to be firmly rejected.

The Fall

Stephen and Alistair explained the presence of evil by the Fall, and it is the belief of most Christians that the world is 'fallen', although many try to reconcile this idea with evolution, because they regard the evidence for some form of evolution to be so strong that it can no more be rejected than belief in a flat earth can be accepted. Even so many academic theologians, who perhaps ought to know better, continue to talk about 'the Fall', as Barbara did. We ought to abandon the word altogether, for it has so many false ideas attached to it.

You will remember that Anne found that she couldn't understand how Barbara was able to speak about 'original sin' when she said she didn't believe in a historical 'fall'. It is indeed very difficult. Part of the reason why people like Barbara retain the term is that Paul's teaching about salvation through the death of Jesus on the cross is set out in terms of a first and second Adam, a fall and redemption. If we stop talking about a fall, then it looks as if the meaning of the cross will be undermined. This, however, is a different question and will have to be discussed in a different book. Here we shall simply note that to many people the very disparity between simply eating the fruit of a tree and the placing of a curse on the whole human race makes the belief incomprehensible.

To other Christians the fact that human beings evolved from earlier forms of life and over many thousands of years makes a literal 'fall' impossible. There never was a time of original innocence from which the original ancestors of the human race fell away by their disobedience.

To others again there is nothing ethical about a transmitted guilt. Indeed it is the very opposite of what they would regard as moral. How, they would say, can anyone be responsible for some sin that a remote ancestor committed? We may be deeply ashamed that the British carried on the slave trade, and may feel it even more deeply because part of the wealth of our country comes from that trade, but we aren't 'guilty' because of that. We may try to make some kind of amends, indeed, we may be guilty today if we do not, but that is quite another matter.

We need, however, to get our ideas straight. To reject a 'fall' doesn't mean that we believe that human beings are born totally innocent and that all that is needed is proper education. The self-centredness, aggression, and cruelty which many people show may well be features of their psychology which were developed through the struggles of evolution. Moreover the early months of the life of human babies, when their very existence depends upon a self-centred demand for food and attention, must increase that self-centredness of our personalities which many regard as the heart of all sin. In a sense, therefore, Barbara was justified in using the term 'original sin', so long as we are careful to remember that it

Two False Trails

doesn't mean that there ever was a time when human beings lived in a happy innocence. It simply expresses the fact that none of us is free from evil thoughts and intentions that result in evil actions.

Genesis 3 has played a quite excessive part in Christian ideas about evil, and we need to put it in its proper place. We shall see a further side to the idea of a 'fall' when we look at natural evils.

Questions to ponder and discuss

1. Why do you think the author calls suffering as a punishment for sin a 'false trail'?

2. Consider the modern penal system. What do you think should be done to rapists and murderers? Why do you think that? Do your ideas about crime and punishment alter your ideas about suffering as divine punishment for sin?

3. The author also called the doctrine of the Fall a 'false trail', yet many Christians regard it as the basis of the Christian gospel. Why do you think he is so opposed to the belief? Why is it so important to many other Christians?

17

The Freewill Defence

Moral evil is easier to deal with than natural evils, although there is no easy answer to either, and we will consider it first.

One answer to the problem of evil which has had a very long history and has been widely accepted by theologians and philosophers is what has come to be known as the 'freewill defence'. In the simplest terms it states that God desired to create human beings who were completely free – free to choose good and free to worship and love him. But freewill carries an enormous risk. For no one is completely free if he or she is unable to choose to do evil and not good. It was a risk God decided to take – and sadly many, perhaps all, human beings choose evil for some or part of the time. Old George Grant's murder, therefore, doesn't constitute a fatal argument against the existence of a loving God, because the men who tortured and killed him were evil. That is the price of giving human beings freedom.

So far so good. But serious problems remain.

In the first place it doesn't get God off the hook. He is still responsible for creating human beings who can choose to do evil. So that *ultimately* he was responsible for George's death.

It might be said in reply that this was a risk that God took because he valued free human beings above all else, and believed that this supreme good was worth paying the price of some evil. But was the price too high? When we consider the destruction, cruelty, murder, rape, other evils that have occurred throughout human history, when we look at the wars that have been waged, the races that have been annihilated, the countless men and women who have toiled as slaves, the many animals that have suffered at the hands of human beings, we cannot avoid asking whether God didn't get his priorities wrong.

The Freewill Defence

Alternatively we might ask whether God had fully anticipated the evil that men and women would wreak in the world. This is to question his omniscience, but it might be claimed that God chose to limit his knowledge when he decided to create free human beings. Certainly to give them freedom to choose how they would act might appear to involve God in giving up some of his power and knowledge of the future. The question of whether it was worth the cost in suffering won't go away.

But perhaps we are wrong in supposing that freewill necessarily means that no one, not even God, knows what an individual is going to choose or how he or she will behave. Anne argued that God ought to have created human beings who had freewill but who nevertheless never chose evil. She pointed out that the best of men and women are extremely predictable. Their goodness of character means that you know how they will act in a given situation, and you discover that they almost always do what you anticipated. If we can 'predict' what a few people will do (which seems to mean that their actions are somehow determined beforehand), surely it would have been possible for God to have made everyone like that. They would be free, but also good.

To some of us this seems to be illogical. True freedom means that the individual can do whatever he or she wants to do at any particular moment. There are no constraints. Those good men and women who always choose the good do so because that is their character. But who formed their character? Surely it was the men and women themselves. They were the ones who built up their characters – and they were free to build that character up as they chose. To have created beings who would always choose right would appear to produce puppets, automatons, creatures controlled by their genes, and certainly not human beings as we know them.

We are, nevertheless, all controlled by our genes and by our upbringing more than we care to admit. It might be, therefore, that these 'free' beings who never choose evil and never inflict pain on anyone or anything wouldn't be so very different from ourselves.

At this point we need to introduce evolution again. Our genes and our dispositions developed, as we have seen, on the one hand through the evolutionary process which lies behind us and on the other through the personal psychological development which we went through in our early life. So we aren't completely free. We are what we are partly because of the long history of animal life and the long period when we were dependent on our parents for food and protection. But it looks as if the very method of creation which the universe has undergone inevitably produced creatures such as the (often evil) human beings which inhabit our planet today.

There is a practical question about the making of the kind of people, the men and women who were free but never chose evil, that Anne desired, as well as the logical one. It seems that a completely different way of creating the world would be needed. We may not be able to imagine how the job might have been done, but it is clear that the way of evolution was unlikely to lead to men and women who always chose what is good for other people and for the world of nature. God could, of course, have chosen that. And the fact that he didn't do so is a further reason why we cannot remove him from all blame for the evil and suffering in the world.

So while the freewill defence offers an *explanation* of some of the evil in the world, it doesn't *excuse* God, and to that extent it might be regarded as not fully adequate. We can always continue to ask, 'Was it worth it?'

It would be much easier to follow David, the reluctant atheist, who accepted that this is how things are. No one is to blame for them. Our task is to try to make the world the least horrible that we can.

The Freewill Defence

Questions to ponder and discuss

1. Try to think through the 'freewill defence'. Does it really explain the problem of evil? What would you say to someone who said that God was still responsible because he created human beings as they are?

2. Anne argued that God should have created human beings who were unable to commit evil. Do you think that this was possible? What kind of people would they have been?

3. Part of the argument seems to be that evolution has produced creatures who are biased (inevitably) towards being self-centred and towards practising evil. Discuss why this is.

4. Human beings have brought great suffering upon each other and have destroyed much of the beauty of the world. Collect examples of the evils that they have brought into the world. Was the creation of men and women worth the price?

5. One way to escape the conclusion that God is responsible for the evil that men and women do is to say that he didn't foresee that they would choose evil in this way. This means that he is not omniscient. Consider whether it is necessary for God to be all-knowing if he is to be God.

18

Natural Evils

Our story contained three kinds of natural evils. Simon was born disabled, Frances developed cancer, and Tom's son John was killed by an earthquake. In addition there were children who had died young and who were buried by grieving parents in the churchyard that Anne's footpath went across. Although they look different, essentially they are the same. They all occur because this is the kind of physical world that we inhabit. It is a world where most children are born healthy, but many are born with disabilities and deformities. It is a world where animals and human beings suffer from diseases, some of which we have learnt to cure, but others still evade medical science. And the very fact that we live in a physical world means that our fragile bodies will be cut, crushed, and injured in many different ways.

Anne complained that God might have created a world in which such pain and suffering could not occur, and she wondered why we have to live in a physical world at all if our ultimate destiny is spiritual. Part of the answer to this might be that character and faith can only be built up in a world like ours. We need to have the opportunity to take moral decisions and to trust in a God whom we cannot see. We shall come back to this later.

But the fact is that if we are to have a physical world, then it is difficult to see how it could be much different from the one we live in. We need a world which is orderly and regular. Without regularity science would be impossible. Without regularity we wouldn't be able to plan for tomorrow. Without things being regular and stable learning would be impossible. We need to be sure that the sun will rise each morning, that the air will continue to have sufficient oxygen to keep us alive, that bread will not suddenly become poisonous, that gravity will not suddenly stop so that we go flying off the earth. A physical

Natural Evils

world can only be our kind of world – and that means that natural disasters will happen. Earthquakes will occur because of tension that builds up along faults in the rocks. Storms will often bring flooding, and drought will occur because the rains fail. Badly built houses will collapse and injure or kill those living in them. The child who eats a poisonous plant will die. Two cars cannot be on the same piece of road without injury to the people in them. This is simply the consequence of our kind of world. It raises the question, Did God *have to* create this kind of world? Or to put it in another way, Is this the best of all worlds?

Then we need to pay attention to what Dr MacLaren said about pain. It is not an *absolute* evil. Without pain we would be likely to injure ourselves seriously. Pain acts as a warning of danger. But this isn't a complete answer, because much pain appears senseless and without any purpose. The degree of pain isn't always in proportion to the seriousness of the disease. And, as he pointed out, before modern medical knowledge and surgical techniques the pain was often useless. Even if we can understand and accept some pain, therefore, this only partly relieves the problem. God is still left with a large amount of pain that has no purpose – and Camus's Dr Rieux would say that that isn't far distant from torture.

Stephen and his friends explained natural evil by saying that the Fall infected nature as well as the human race. This has been a traditional Christian belief, but today it looks extremely vulnerable. We have seen that the whole idea of a 'fall' from an original innocence is, quite frankly, incredible. The universe evolved from an original single unit of energy, and nebulae and stars eventually condensed out. On our own planet plants, animals and human beings all evolved over millions of years. There is no place for a 'fall' from an original innocence. And in any case almost as far back as we can go, we have evidence that human beings attacked and killed each other – look at the effort that was put into building defensive fortifications.

Beyond this, it is difficult to see how a single act of disobedience by human beings could have distorted the whole of the universe (for the infection of sin would have to reach beyond our planet, which is part of the entire universe, in which the same physical laws run). Plants and animals existed before human beings, and the consequence of the Fall could hardly be retrospective. It is difficult not to conclude that the belief in natural evil being the consequence of the Fall is a hangover from a pre-scientific age, which hasn't been fully thought out. It must be abandoned.

We are left then with the fact that our world came into being as part of the evolution of the universe, and that it is the kind of world that it is because that is the kind of universe of which it is a part. To argue, therefore, that God should have created a different world for us to live in means that we are questioning the goodness of the entire universe. Apart from the question of whether a different kind of universe is possible, it would appear that we have either to take the physical world as being all there is, or accept by faith that this is the best world for God's purposes. David took the first way, and tried to relieve the suffering that he found in it as far as he was able. But like Anne, we want to believe in God, but believe with a good conscience. So we must puzzle our way forward a bit further.

We have already rejected Anne's suggestion that perhaps God himself was limited by the physical matter with which he was working, because it relieves him from blame for the natural evils in the world, but only at the cost of his omnipotence. He wouldn't be the sole eternal being, for the physical universe would also exist alongside of him and independently of him. Nor would he be in complete control of everything.

We looked more favourably at the slightly modified version of Anne's suggestion, that God limited himself voluntarily when he decided to create the universe through the means of evolution. There are two ways of envisaging this.

Natural Evils

In one version he just started it off and then let it run its course. He would still be *ultimately* responsible for the evils in the world, but only in so far as he failed to foresee that this might happen, or because he knew that this was a possibility and accepted the risk.

In the other form of the theory, God can still be pictured as in control, not by 'interfering' with the natural processes (that view is untenable in the face of a scientific understanding of the way the universe runs) but by co-operating with these laws. In this case his involvement in the evil in the world is greater, for we can ask why he didn't work with the laws more often or more effectively, and in this way prevent the massive natural evils that we find. On this view the pressure to demand whether it was worth the cost of the massive suffering across the millennia is much greater.

This, indeed, is the fundamental question which we have had to face. Was it worth the price? Many would answer 'No', and either abandon religion or fight against the God whom they see to be malign. You will recall that Dr MacLaren said that he sometimes felt that he was working against God by trying to set a faulty universe right. It is certainly a question which we can neither evade nor treat lightly.

Before we leave this question, however, a little more needs to be said about the suffering of animals. First, we need to ask whether animals can suffer. There have been philosophers who have denied that they can, but our bodies are very similar to those of animals, and animals react to injuries in the same way that we would, and this makes it certain that they can feel pain. C. S. Lewis suggested that the suffering of animals was far less than ours because they neither anticipate pain nor are consciously aware that they are suffering. (He also believed that their suffering is due to human sin, but we have already seen that this is difficult to accept.) Today there must be very few people who would say that animals do not feel pain, even though they probably don't know the fear of death, which is

Why Evil and Suffering?

one of the greatest forms of suffering that we have to endure. It is true that some animals appear to grieve over the death of their mate or their young just as we do, but they can hardly be supposed to wonder what will happen to them after they have been killed. So animals *do* feel pain, even if their suffering may be less than ours in some ways.

Then we need to reckon up the extent of animal pain. Some animal pain is the result of human cruelty, and this can be met with the 'freewill defence', an explanation that is as strong or weak as we hold that defence to be. But we are still left with three unpalatable kinds of animal suffering: (1) most of the animals are the prey of predators, and killing appears to be a central part of the natural world; (2) even if we leave this out of account, animals are still killed by natural disasters, such as lightning, earthquake, flood, drought, falling from cliffs or being crushed by rocks; and (3) animals are attacked by diseases in exactly the same way as human beings are. Some people are troubled even more by the vast 'waste' that is a necessary feature of evolution, since many millions of creatures die (and have to die for evolution to 'work') before they become adult and many species – and not just dinosaurs! – evolve and then become extinct. So it seems that many individuals and many whole species serve no purpose except to make the evolution of other species possible.

Once again the underlying doubt remains: is the creation of men and women worth the cost of all this suffering and destruction?

It needs, however, to be kept in a certain perspective. We ought not to fasten so exclusively upon the pain and suffering in the world that we overlook the beauty, happiness, and goodness that we find in it. Flowers are beautiful. Birdsong does delight us. We can enjoy the physical sensations of wind or water on our bodies. Friendships are good. We could collect a very long catalogue of things that make life in our world worthwhile. The woman who watches her baby starving to

Natural Evils

death, however, isn't likely to appreciate the starlit heavens. Those whose loved-ones are buried in a house shattered by an earthquake are not likely to spend time gazing at the flowers in the garden. We need to maintain a sense of proportion between the evils and the good, but in the end we have to let the good go and ask whether the pain is serving any purpose. One purpose might be to develop human character, and we turn to this in the next chapter.

Questions to ponder and discuss

1. Is this 'the best of all worlds'? Collect up the things that are good about it. What kind of a world might a better world be like?

2. In what ways is it possible to think that God limited himself in creating the world? Does this make him less than God?

3. Dorothee Soelle has said that in the light of the suffering that there is in the world it is impossible to hold simultaneously that God is omnipotent, all-loving, and comprehensible. What do you think she meant?

4. How far do you think that the suffering of animals is a strong argument against the goodness (or even the existence) of God?

5. Alfred Tennyson was greatly troubled by the thought that so many species had died out (read *In Memoriam*, stanzas LV, LVI). Consider whether the loss of these species is an evil. What questions does evolution raise about the goodness of God?

19

A Vale of Soul-Making

You will recall that some members of Anne's church described our world as 'a vale of soul-making' and she reacted very violently against the idea, recalling the experience of Mrs Jones, whose soul had certainly not been 'made' as a result of her experiences. Despite the difficulties with the idea, it has met considerable favour both among philosophers and with ordinary Christians. (The phrase comes in one of Keats' letters.)

At first sight it seems to provide a complete answer to the problem of suffering. In much the same way that war can produce unexpected virtues of courage, compassion, and self-sacrifice, despite its horror and viciousness, so suffering, either the suffering of the individual herself or of her loved-ones, can bring out similar virtues. Perhaps a man didn't know that he had it in him to act as a patient nurse and carer until his wife had a disabling stroke and he had to look after her. Perhaps a woman who had always been afraid of pain discovers untapped resources of endurance when cancer strikes. The existence of suffering certainly offers opportunities to help one another which would not be there were it not for this evil.

And yet ... Anne certainly has a point. How can suffering and morality be weighed in the balance? How can you compare patience and pain, courage and disability? More seriously, is the massive suffering in the world that overwhelms so many helpless and innocent people a price that can rightly be paid for the virtues that it may awaken in the sufferers or in others? And what of those people who have been simply crushed by their suffering?

Some have tried to meet this question by asserting that God has arranged the world so that suffering is never too great to be borne. When a certain level of pain is reached the sufferer loses consciousness. This is itself doubtful, but even if it were true it would only mean that torture was permitted, but only up to a certain level.

Others have argued that because of the discovery of many pain killers today, we are more sensitive to pain than any previous generation. With a distorted sense of values, we regard pain as a much greater evil than moral wrong. While there may be something in the suggestion that hedonism reigns today, few people would be happy with the idea that pain is in some sense good.

And however we react to these two ways of alleviating the problem, we are still left with the massive suffering of the Jews in Hitler's Germany, and the people like Mrs Jones, who started out by developing strengths of character and new levels of goodness, only to be beaten in the end. There are also those children, like the other Ann, who die long before their souls can have been 'made' and who may have suffered greatly in their short lives.

The accusations of Camus in *The Plague*, and Ivan Karamazov in Dostoyevsky's novel continue to stare out at us. 'Tell me yourself,' says Ivan to his brother Aloysha, 'I challenge you – answer. Imagine that you are creating a fabric of human destiny with the object of making me happy in the end, giving them peace and rest at last, but that it was essential and inevitable to torture to death only one tiny creature – that baby beating its breast with its fist, for instance – and to found that edifice on its unavenged tears, would you consent to be the architect on those conditions?' However lofty the goodness that suffering evokes, however blessed the heaven to which human beings may go, we are still left with the central doubt: was the price worth paying?

So far we have been thinking simply about human beings and the way the suffering they meet develops their characters and enables them to act in heroic and virtuous ways. We saw in the last chapter, however, that even the existence of human life involved the death and suffering of countless other creatures,

Why Evil and Suffering?

and we asked whether it was worth the price to enable men and women to appear on our planet. The question might be pushed a bit further, by asking what was the purpose of creating human beings in this way.

Anne couldn't get away from the idea that it ought to have been possible for God to create a world in which all the good things that we know were present without the suffering that is part of the lot of both human beings and animals in our world. But the fact of evolution makes us ask why it was necessary for so many millions of animals to live and suffer and die so that beings who were capable of choosing good rather than evil and of responding to God without coercion could appear.

To suggest that all the creatures make a contribution to the good of the whole universe and that the joy which they find in life is part of that good which outweighs the pain they have to endure may bring relief to some. Others will be less satisfied and, with Anne, will press the question of why it had to be so. To justify the existence of the animals simply as a means to the creation of human beings appears to place the human race far too much in the centre of the universe, especially when biology points increasingly to our kinship with the animals.

John Hick, who makes out the most convincing case for the idea of a 'vale of soul-making', fails in the end to reach beyond a questioning and a hope. 'Can there be a future good so great as to render acceptable, in retrospect, the whole human experience, with all its wickedness and suffering as well as all its sanctity and happiness? I think that perhaps there can, and indeed perhaps there is.' Anne would still wonder.

A Vale of Soul-Making

Questions to ponder and discuss

1. 'How can suffering and morality be weighed in the balance? How can you compare patience and pain, courage and disability? More seriously, is the massive suffering in the world that overwhelms so many helpless and innocent people a price that can rightly be paid for the virtues that it may awaken in the sufferers or in others?' These were asked as rhetorical questions, but try to answer them.

2. Some of the words of Ivan in *The Brothers Karamazov* were quoted in this chapter. In Camus's *The Plague* a small boy lies dying in agony. The priest Fr Paneloux comments: 'That sort of thing is revolting because it passes our human understanding. But perhaps we should love what we cannot understand.' The atheist Dr Rieux shakes his head. 'No, Father. I've a very different idea of love. And until my dying day I shall refuse to love a scheme of things in which children are put to torture.' What would you reply to Dr Rieux?

3. Is the promise of everlasting happiness in heaven an adequate answer to the problem of suffering in this life? Consider John Hick's question: 'Can there be a future good so great as to render acceptable ... the whole human experience?' Remember that Anne wondered why it was necessary to have a physical life as a prelude to a spiritual one.

20

Does God Intervene?

The members of Anne's church held the prayer vigil for Frances. Anne's attitude to prayer was very different from that of the people who had arranged the vigil. They were convinced that if they prayed hard enough God would cure Frances. The more conservative members of the church which Stephen had joined thought the same, but said that Frances wasn't cured because she lacked faith. Her illness showed that she wasn't a 'real Christian'.

Anne simply wanted to be quiet with God and think about Frances and Stephen. She wasn't sure that God did intervene and heal people, in spite of the stories in the Gospels. Later in our story we found Anne remembering how the church had prayed for Felicity, and yet she had still died.

Prayer is a large topic that will be considered in another book in this series. Here we have to look at the question of whether God does intervene to save people from suffering.

One answer would be to stress the kind of world that science has revealed. Modern scientists no longer believe in iron natural laws which leave no space for divine action. In the very smallest particles in the universe prediction is impossible because they don't seem to be governed by laws. Yet quantum physics and the place that chance seems to have played in the evolution of the universe do not automatically take us back to the times when God was believed to be an actor in human history. Even the scientists who are most sensitive to religion haven't been particularly successful in showing how providence can be imagined intellectually.

Origen in the third century wrote: 'It would be utterly absurd for a man who was troubled by the scorching sun at the summer solstice to imagine that by his prayer the sun could be shifted back to its spring-time place among the heavenly bodies', and a modern theologian has commented that once this principle is accepted it is difficult to put any limit to its scope. The group at Anne's church claimed that their prayer had worked a cure for Frances, but the hospital specialist attributed it to chemotherapy and pointed to the remissions that often occur naturally. If God cannot stop the sun in its tracks, why should we suppose that he can miraculously cure a sick person? It is simply that we know enough about the solar system to be certain that nothing can change the celestial movements. On the other hand, much about disease and human beings is still a mystery to us. This doesn't make the principle any different, however, and we have no reason to suppose that God can intervene there either.

Certainly we ought not to be too worried that we are unable to devise a picture of the working of providence which we find convincing. God is far greater than our small minds and to suppose that we can understand everything about his actions is to make him less than God. But there is still a problem with the idea that God intervenes to help people who pray to him or for whom prayers are said. And it is the moral problem of fairness.

We should ask ourselves, whether we really believe that God cures one person because he or she prayed to him or because they happened to have a group of Christian friends who organized a prayer vigil, when there are many more people who aren't cured? It just won't do to say that there was not enough faith, or they didn't pray hard enough. The failure of God to do anything when six million Jews died in the Nazi crematoria is a warning against adopting easy beliefs. Many of them died with the *Shema'* ('Hear, O Israel, the LORD is one . . .') on their lips.

The world isn't a fair place. That is obvious. The child born in Ethiopia stands far less chance of even surviving into adulthood, let alone enjoying a comfortable and rich life, than the child born to a middle-class family in the south of England. And disease and accident are no respecters of goodness. The problem with the idea that God adjusts some of the evil in the world by actively intervening and occasionally answering

Why Evil and Suffering?

prayers is that his actions are increasing the unfairness instead of rectifying it. There appears to be no answer to the question of why one person recovers and another dies.

It is the immorality of unfair treatment which is the main objection to a belief that God intervenes and heals the sufferer who prays to him.

We must leave this here and refer the reader to that other volume in this series, but there is a little more to say as far as the problem of suffering goes. We thought earlier about the way God limited his power when he created men and women who were free to reject his love and do evil things. Now it seems that by creating our kind of universe God limited himself in another way. He created a world from which he stood back and allowed evolution to do its work, even when that evolution produced germs, viruses and cancers. And when those viruses and cancers did bring illness and suffering, he still stood back and left human beings to discover how to cure them.

Anne would no doubt say that when he discovered that these evils had been produced within his universe, he ought to have stepped in and either halted the whole process or made an adjustment so that they were prevented from harming human beings and animals. But this is how it seems to be.

Some people will now ask, 'But if God stands back and doesn't intervene, then isn't that the same as there being no God at all?' We shall have to consider this later on.

Does God Intervene?

Questions to ponder and discuss

1. If it is absurd to pray for the sun to be shifted lower in the sky during the summer, why is it not absurd to pray for someone who is ill? (Or perhaps it is absurd?)

2. One of the main arguments in this chapter is that some of the claims of healing make God appear to be acting unfairly, healing some people and allowing others to suffer and die. How would you meet this charge?

3. 'The child born in Ethiopia stands far less chance of even surviving into adulthood, let alone enjoying a comfortable and rich life, than the child born to a middle-class family in the south of England.' How can you explain the general unfairness in the distribution of individual talents and material goods in the world?

4. Why do you think God allowed germs, viruses and cancers to develop in his universe?

21

People Before Doctrine

It is time to go back to Stephen. He was devastated by his wife's cancer – so completely crushed that he abandoned all belief. It showed to Anne a new side of his character and she even said that she was glad that he had lost his faith. That may not have been the right response, and yet we can understand why she said it. The reason came out even more clearly when she complained that the group of rigid believers placed correct doctrine before caring for people. And that, we saw, was the error which Job's friends fell into in the Old Testament.

Throughout our story we have seen how important it is to go behind the problem of evil to the people who are suffering. How they feel matters more than finding a right answer to suffering as an intellectual problem. It is worth thinking about this a bit more.

The problem of evil meets us in different ways. To the person who is in rude good health it may be an absorbing intellectual puzzle. To the woman who has just been told that she has cancer and probably has only two more years to live it may raise the question 'Why me?' or even induce a sense of guilt, as it did in Frances. The reaction of the man who looks after his wife who has had a stroke and who has to care for her in most intimate ways may be either to rail against God or hardly to notice that there is a problem of suffering. His only concern is to see what he can do to make his wife's life happier. Young Ann's parents who put up that tombstone may have found that to think of her as one of God's angels enabled them to bear their grief.

This means that the woman who read a tract to Stephen and Frances showed such a lack of love and understanding that her action was almost unforgivable. And it shows us that the first thing we need to do when suffering comes to anyone we know is to bring sympathy. Stephen found that it was a great help just to be able to pour out his feelings to Anne, even though she herself felt she had done nothing.

We have thought about this as a problem of personal relationship and caring, but it has a relevance for the specific problem of evil. It shows us that there is more to the matter than finding a solution to a philosophical problem that will satisfy our minds. To wrestle with the intellectual problem is important, and we have spent most of our time dealing with it. But we miss our way if we remain on a purely intellectual level. For suffering is a matter of people. It was Stephen and Frances and Tom and the rest who suffered, and the first thing that their friends had to do was to try to share their anguish, impossible as that was. Job's friends showed themselves to be real friends when they came to where he was, on the ash heaps outside the village, and just sat with him in silence for seven days.

And God's actions in creating the universe, with all its consequences, are not just the actions of an unchanging and impassive deity but for the Christian they are the actions of the one whom Jesus addressed as Father.

This is where Fred comes in. He held a firm faith in the Bible and in Jesus. If he was challenged he would tell you that we are all sinners and Jesus died on the cross to save us all. But he was humane with his conservative faith. He loved his Lord and he loved people. So he knew when to speak and when to be silent. He would offer a helping hand as well as tell people about Jesus, and he knew when it was appropriate to do either. He was so different from the people in the church which Stephen had joined.

On the human level, then, the first thing for the individual to do is to try to relieve suffering, to combat evil, and to help produce a society in which there is less inequality and where those who have least chance and are the least able to cope with all that life brings them are given the greatest help and care. Fred and Dr Mac show us the way.

Why Evil and Suffering?

From the side of God it leads us to ask, 'How does he react to the suffering which occurs in the world he has made?' But that will require a whole chapter.

Questions to ponder and discuss

1. If people matter before right doctrine, what place has doctrine in the Christian life? (Think about some of the characters in our story. Stephen's friends, who sincerely believe that unless an individual has faith in the cross he or she will go to hell. Fred, who loves his Bible, believes that the sacrifice of Jesus on the cross forgives sins, and yet cares for people. Dr Mac, who devoted his life to healing people, even though it seemed to him at times that he was fighting against God. And Geoff, who sometimes appeared to regard solving the problem of suffering as a game, and yet who had a deep faith in God that controlled his life.)

2. Consider whether it matters that some people adopt beliefs that are clearly false, provided that faith helps them to deal with their suffering.

3. Stephen lost his faith because it was so rigid that it couldn't cope with Frances' cancer. What does this tell us about faith – and love?

22

A Suffering God?

Traditional Christian theology took over from Greek philosophy the idea that God cannot suffer. We can appreciate why the early Christian thinkers believed this. God had to be perfect. But then, they asked, how could someone who suffered be perfect? It would mean that what other people did could affect him. It would also mean that he changed from being a God of supreme blessedness and joy to one who suffered. So it seemed to make him less than God.

In modern times theologians have come to see that the idea of a God whose perfection meant that he could not change made him less than God. They have come to realize that if he loves the creatures he has made, this must necessarily involve him in suffering when they suffer. More than that, it means that he is willing to suffer for them and by their side. He was most himself when he entered our world in Jesus and shared our life and our pains. Through the cross he endures the sufferings which are an inevitable part of the kind of universe he created.

Many sermons have been preached in which what the preacher said can be expressed in five simple sentences: 'I can give you no explanation of the *meaning* of suffering. All I can do is to point you to the cross which lies eternally in the heart of God. For although God created a world in which men and women suffer, he didn't remain outside, watching our writhings. He came into our world and shared our sufferings. And he still shares them.'

We may say that that isn't sufficient for us. It is all very well to push the problem to one side and affirm that a God who made a world which seems to be so grievously flawed nevertheless shares in the consequences of his action. This certainly defends his goodness. But what about his omnipotence and his omniscience? Doesn't it make him too feeble to be God? Doesn't it mean that he is unable to help us?

Why Evil and Suffering?

As one writer put it, 'If I have fallen into a well, I don't want someone to climb down and just sit with me, I want someone with a ladder and a rope to pull me out.'

Even if we accept the idea that God joins with all the creatures he has made in paying the price, we still want to ask whether the price is not too high. Ivan's question won't go away, and it may well be that there is no answer to it. All that we can do is to take the leap of faith, accepting that God may have had a purpose which we cannot understand, and being willing to trust him.

This is why we have so much sympathy with David, who is the unwilling unbeliever. He longs for God. He never stops seeking the way to faith. But he is not willing to sacrifice his moral integrity. Life is a sorry show, and he will do all he can to right what is wrong, to ease suffering, and to share the pain of those who are struck down. But he will not believe what he cannot intellectually accept. It is also why we warm towards Dr MacLaren, who devoted his whole life to the work of healing, even if sometimes he feels that he is struggling across the grain of the universe and fighting against God. Better to be honest than to adopt a warped and twisted creed.

It is also why it is important to read the book of Job and some of the Psalms. For there we find men who argued with God, accused him of cruelty and tyranny, asked why he remained silent and inactive, challenged him as to his goodness. Today we have many accounts of people who were at the end of their tether. They shouted their accusations at a God whom they didn't believe in. And then, strangely, at that moment of defiance and despair they found that God was real to them, and they began to see a way of rebuilding their lives.

This is why the concept of the vale of soul-making is no complete answer. The price is too high, and the losers are too many. It only fits into place if God's soul also has to be made in the vale.

But then another price has to be paid.

A Suffering God?

Part of that price must go to pay for the loss of traditional Western Christianity. This God is no longer changeless, no longer the God who cannot suffer. No longer does the idea of a Fall provide an answer. No longer do we find a God who can intervene to save his servants from suffering when they pray to him. Isn't this being too powerless to be God?

Part of the price must be the very concept of God. What kind of a *God* is it who makes our kind of universe and then has to make atonement for his own errors? Isn't this being too incompetent to be God?

We might pay a different kind of price. A being who is worthy of the name of God must be far beyond all human thought and imagining. We may, therefore, pay the price of our own inability to find an answer. Geoff was rightly hesitant about accepting this way through, and Anne bluntly rejected the idea of the mysterious ways by which God works his wonders. We ought to respect their intellectual integrity. To abandon that is too great a price. And yet we cannot expect to understand God's mind as if we were greater than he. In every attempt to deal with the problem of suffering a sense of human ignorance and God's greatness remains.

There is no limit to our questions, but in the end we may find that all we can do when suffering comes is to look at Jesus and trust in his love.

Questions to ponder and discuss

1. If God suffers, does that mean he is less than perfect?

2. If we admit in the end that we cannot provide an answer to the problem of suffering, does that mean that our Christian life is based on a 'sheer leap of blind faith'? And if so, how is that any better than a 'sheer leap of blind doubt'?

Why Evil and Suffering?

3. In what ways does the life and death of Jesus help us to cope with evil and suffering?

4. Think about the 'five sentences' of the preacher (p. 93). Are they sufficient for the Christian or can anything more be said?

Further Reading

Peter Vardy, *The Puzzle of Evil*, Fount, HarperCollins 1992, ISBN 0-00-627638-5.

This is probably the best book to go to after finishing this study. Peter Vardy writes extremely clearly, and gives summaries at the end of each chapter. His approach is important because he deals first with the problem of evil, and stresses the extreme difficulty of finding an answer by reason alone. He then considers 'The Mystery of Evil', concludes that we have to combat evil, and takes a leap of faith.

John Hick, *Evil and the God of Love*, Macmillan 1966, 2nd edition 1977, ISBN 0-333-19672-4.

This is a large scale discussion, but do not be afraid of the 'big book', which often gives the writer an opportunity to expand his or her ideas and so is easy to read. Hick sets out two traditional Christian ways of answering the problem of evil and then presents his own proposal. Get the book out of the library and read Part IV: A Theodicy for Today.

Kenneth Surin, *Theology and the Problem of Evil*, Blackwell 1986, ISBN 0-631-14664-4.

Surin points to two kinds of answers to the problem, theoretical and practical. He thinks the latter fare better, but his own view is that the only answer which can stand up to the suffering of Auschwitz and meet the criticisms of atheism is one based on God's action. 'The Christian who takes the atonement seriously has no real need for theodicy.' It is not an easy book to read, but is probably the most spiritually sensitive. Surin's integrity shines through.

Further Reading

Stephen T. Davis (ed), *Encountering Evil*, John Knox/T&T Clark 1981, ISBN 0-567-29107-3.

Five philosophers and theologians present their own attempts to grapple with the problem of suffering and evil, and these are then opened up to discussion.

Dorothee Soelle, *Theology for Sceptics*, Mowbray 1995, ISBN 0-264-67333-6.

Dorothee Soelle is one of the leading German feminist theologians. This is a very accessible and honest book, which faces up to such evils as Auschwitz. Do not be put off by stock feminist assertions. She links God's suffering with ours, and among her many illustrations is a quotation from the great mediaeval mystic Meister Eckhart and an account of the work of Pater Alfredo, a priest in Guatemala.

Ruth Page, *God and the Web of Creation*, SCM Press 1996, ISBN 0-334-02653-9.

While not directly on the problem of evil and suffering, this is a superb study of the relation of God to the world. Ruth Page fearlessly tackles the problems raised by modern knowledge and opens up many new ways of thinking about God, creation, providence, and the world in which we live. It is especially valuable in taking into account non-human creation, thus widening the range of thinking about sin and suffering.

The novelists have as much to offer us as the theologians and philosophers. Camus's *The Plague* and Dostoyevsky's *The Brothers Karamazov* are essential reading.